HAL•LEONARD®

GUITAR PLAY-ALONG

AUDIO ACCESS INCLUDED

VOL. 107

CREAM

T0084180

PLAYBACK+
Speed • Pitch • Balance • Loop

To access audio visit:
www.halleonard.com/mylibrary

1986-4661-0190-5947

Cover photo: © Jan Persson / Redferns / Getty Images

ISBN 978-1-4234-6975-9

7777 W. BLUEMOUND RD. P.O. BOX 13819 MILWAUKEE, WI 53213

Visit Hal Leonard Online at
www.halleonard.com

Guitar Notation Legend

THE MUSICAL STAFF shows pitches and rhythms and is divided by bar lines into measures. Pitches are named after the first seven letters of the alphabet.

TABLATURE graphically represents the guitar fingerboard. Each horizontal line represents a string, and each number represents a fret.

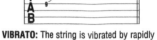

Notes:

Strings:
high E
B
G
D
A
low E

4th string, 2nd fret

1st & 2nd strings open, played together

open D chord

HALF-STEP BEND: Strike the note and bend up 1/2 step.

WHOLE-STEP BEND: Strike the note and bend up one step.

GRACE NOTE BEND: Strike the note and immediately bend up as indicated.

SLIGHT (MICROTONE) BEND: Strike the note and bend up 1/4 step.

BEND AND RELEASE: Strike the note and bend up as indicated, then release back to the original note. Only the first note is struck.

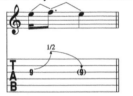

PRE-BEND: Bend the note as indicated, then strike it.

VIBRATO: The string is vibrated by rapidly bending and releasing the note with the fretting hand.

PALM MUTING: The note is partially muted by the pick hand lightly touching the string(s) just before the bridge.

HAMMER-ON: Strike the first (lower) note with one finger, then sound the higher note (on the same string) with another finger by fretting it without picking.

PULL-OFF: Place both fingers on the notes to be sounded. Strike the first note and without picking, pull the finger off to sound the second (lower) note.

LEGATO SLIDE: Strike the first note and then slide the same fret-hand finger up or down to the second note. The second note is not struck.

SHIFT SLIDE: Same as legato slide, except the second note is struck.

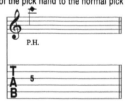

TRILL: Very rapidly alternate between the notes indicated by continuously hammering on and pulling off.

TAPPING: Hammer ("tap") the fret indicated with the pick-hand index or middle finger and pull off to the note fretted by the fret hand.

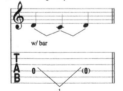

NATURAL HARMONIC: Strike the note while the fret-hand lightly touches the string directly over the fret indicated.

PINCH HARMONIC: The note is fretted normally and a harmonic is produced by adding the edge of the thumb or the tip of the index finger of the pick hand to the normal pick attack.

TREMOLO PICKING: The note is picked as rapidly and continuously as possible.

VIBRATO BAR DIVE AND RETURN: The pitch of the note or chord is dropped a specified number of steps (in rhythm), then returned to the original pitch.

VIBRATO BAR SCOOP: Depress the bar just before striking the note, then quickly release the bar.

VIBRATO BAR DIP: Strike the note and then immediately drop a specified number of steps, then release back to the original pitch.

Additional Musical Definitions

(accent) • Accentuate note (play it louder).

(staccato) • Play the note short.

D.S. al Coda • Go back to the sign (𝄋), then play until the measure marked "*To Coda*," then skip to the section labelled "Coda."

D.C. al Fine • Go back to the beginning of the song and play until the measure marked "*Fine*" (end).

Fill

N.C.

• Label used to identify a brief melodic figure which is to be inserted into the arrangement.

• Harmony is implied.

• Repeat measures between signs.

• When a repeated section has different endings, play the first ending only the first time and the second ending only the second time.

1. 2.

HAL•LEONARD®
GUITAR
PLAY-ALONG
AUDIO
ACCESS
INCLUDED

CONTENTS

Page	Title
4	Badge
10	Cross Road Blues (Crossroads)
24	Politician
34	Spoonful
48	Strange Brew
19	Sunshine of Your Love
56	Tales of Brave Ulysses
64	White Room

Badge

Words and Music by Eric Clapton and George Harrison

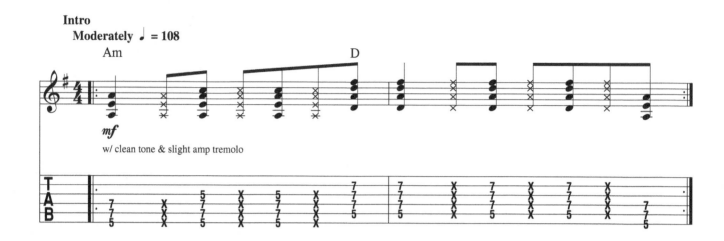

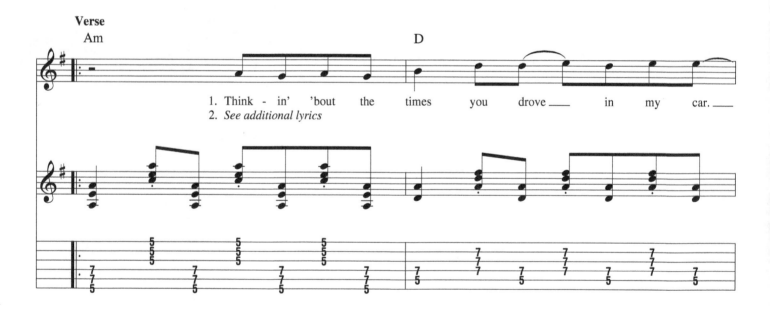

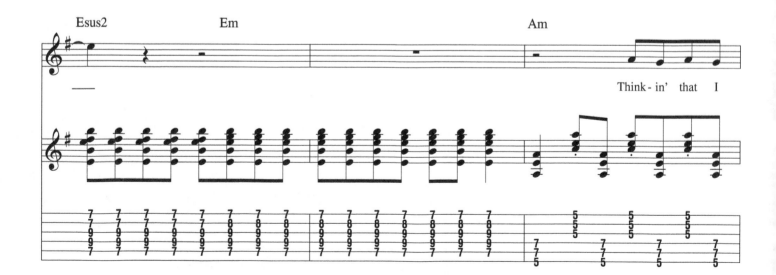

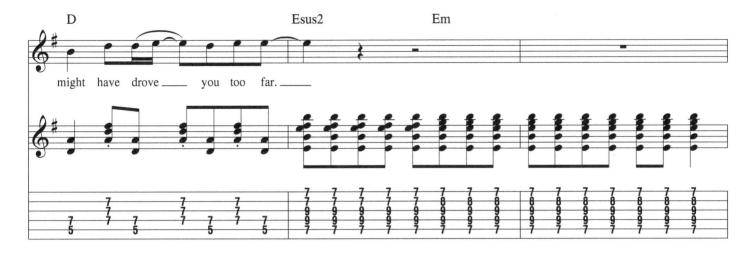

might have drove ____ you too far. ____

And I'm think-in' 'bout the love that you made on my ta - ble.

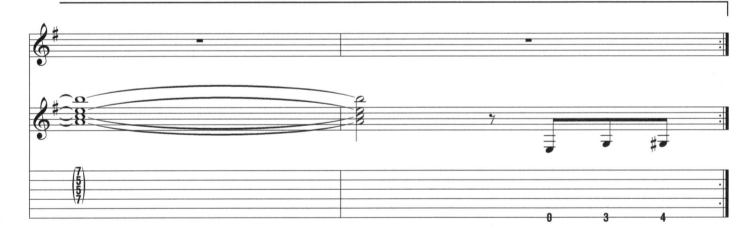

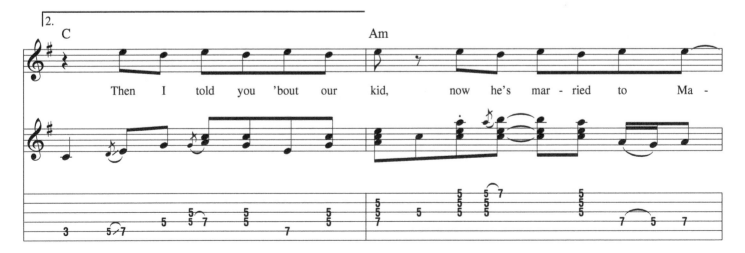

Then I told you 'bout our kid, now he's mar - ried to Ma -

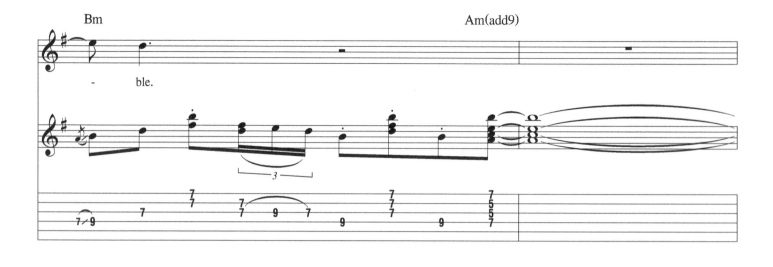

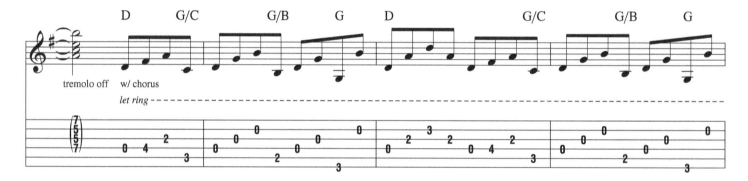

Bridge

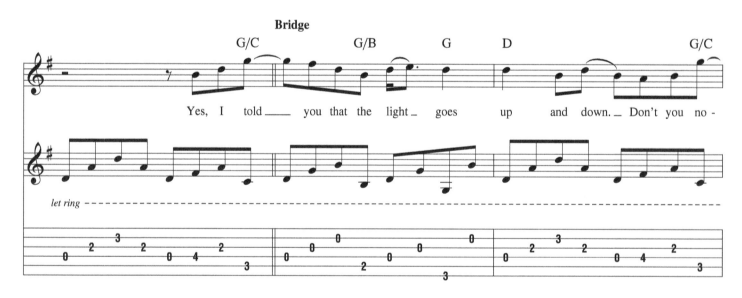

Yes, I told ____ you that the light _ goes up and down. _ Don't you no -

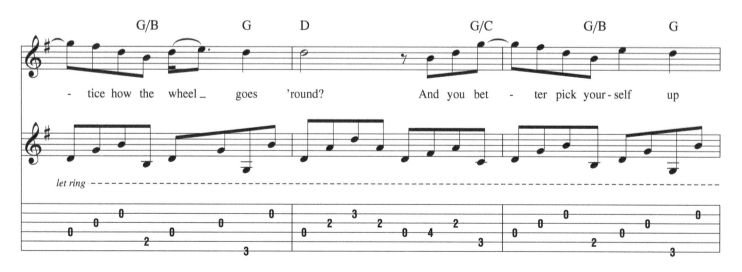

- tice how the wheel _ goes 'round? And you bet - ter pick your - self up

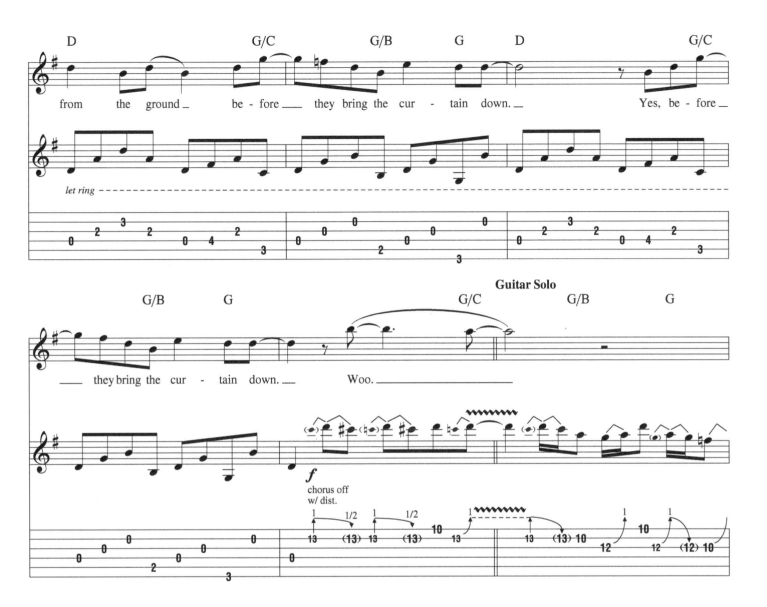

from the ground __ be - fore __ they bring the cur - tain down. __

Yes, be - fore __

let ring -

Guitar Solo

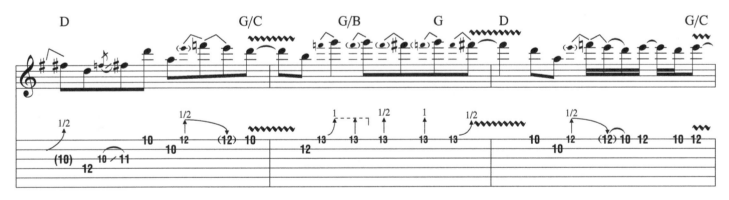

__ they bring the cur - tain down. __

Woo. _____

chorus off
w/ dist.

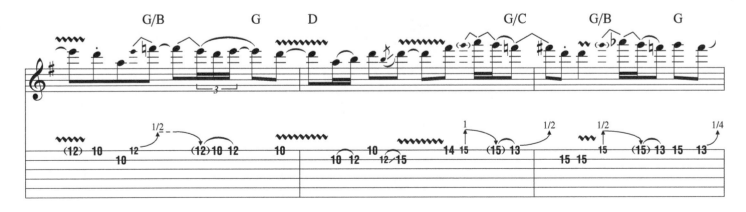

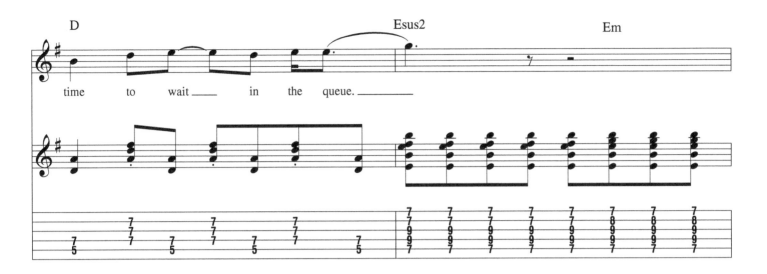

time to wait ___ in the queue. ___

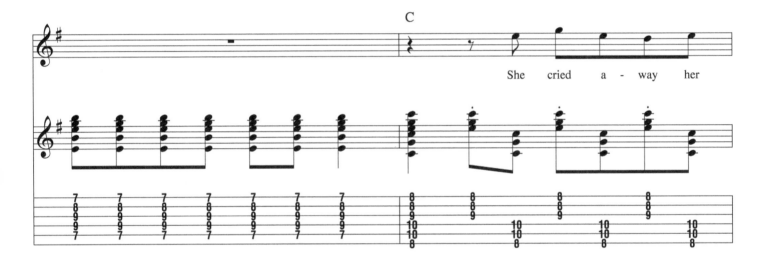

She cried a - way her

life since she fell off the cra - dle.

Additional Lyrics

2. I told you not to wander 'round in the dark.
   I told you 'bout the swans, that they live in the park.
   Then I told you 'bout our kid now he's married to Mable.

Cross Road Blues
(Crossroads)

Words and Music by Robert Johnson

Intro
Moderately fast Rock ♩ = 130

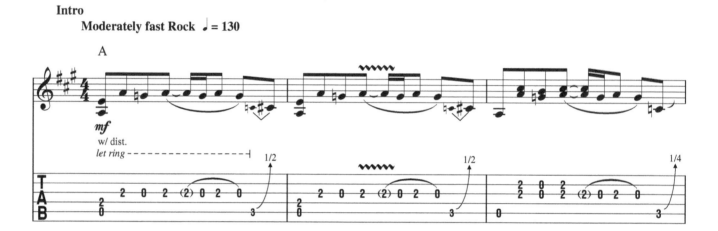

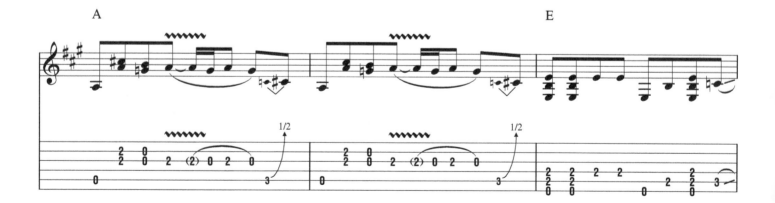

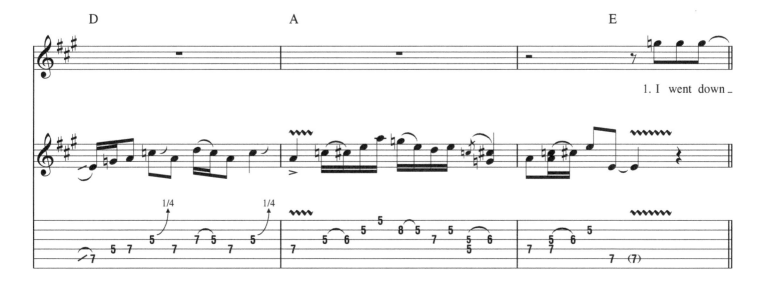

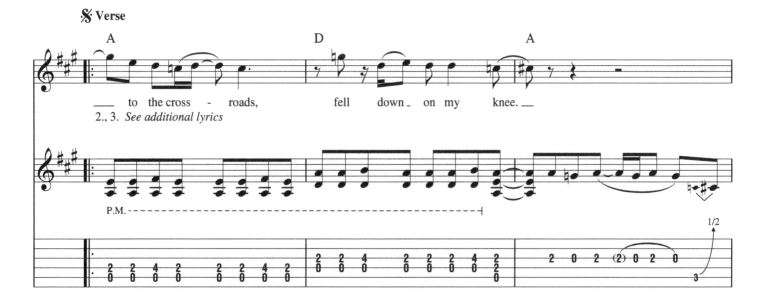

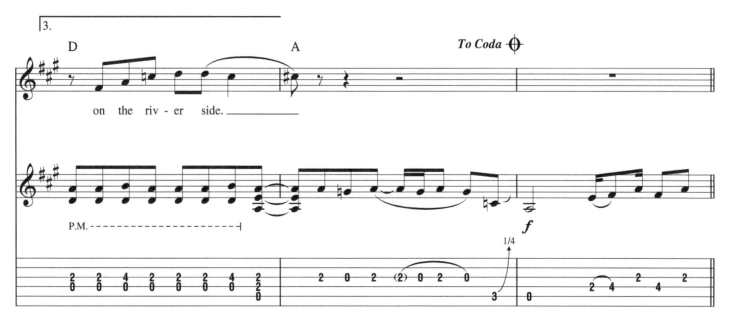

Guitar Solo

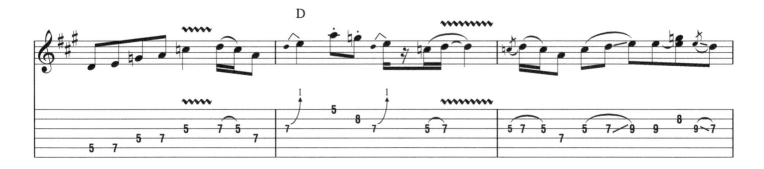

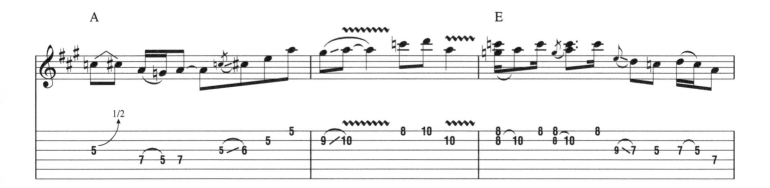

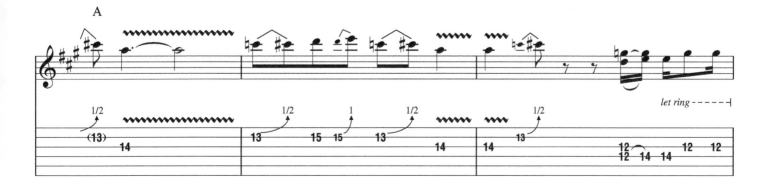

D

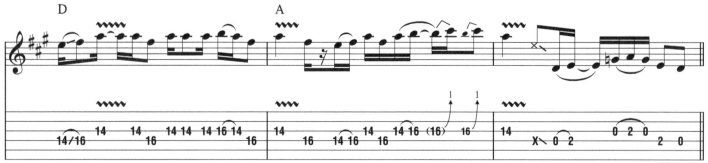

A
E

D.S. al Coda
(3rd Verse, 3rd ending)

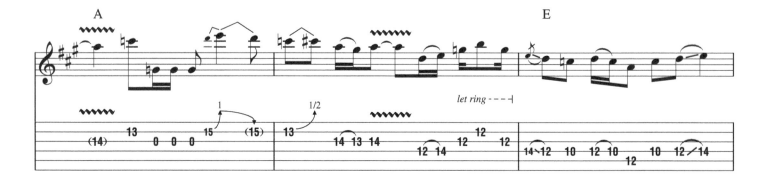

D
A

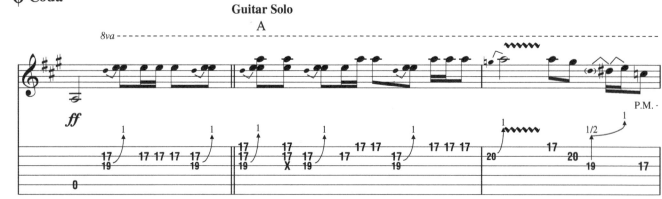

Coda

Guitar Solo

A

8va

ff

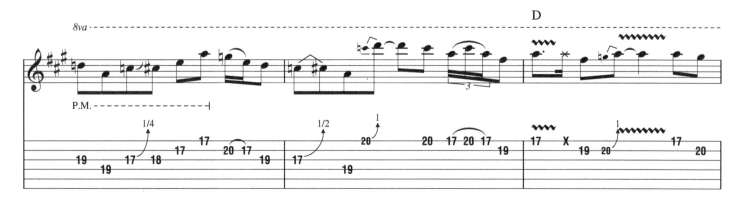

8va

D

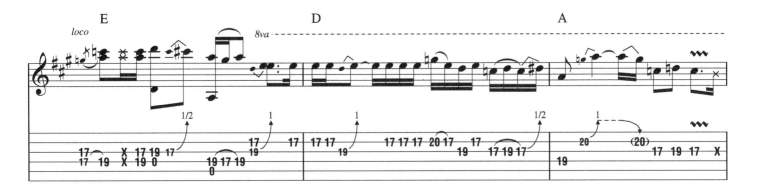

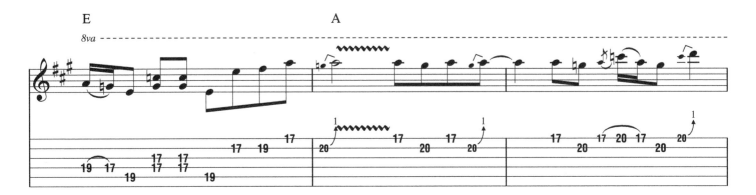

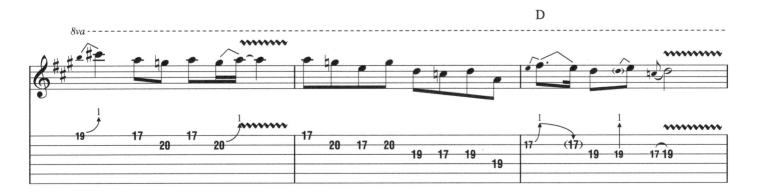

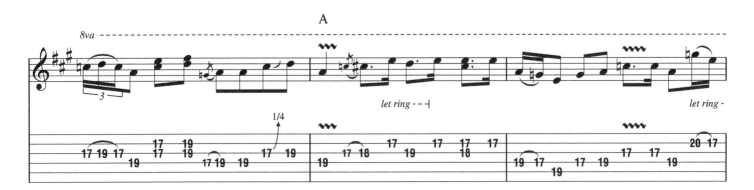

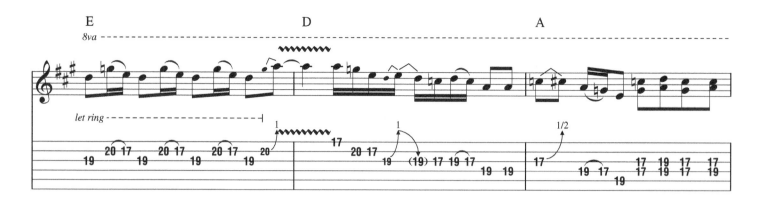

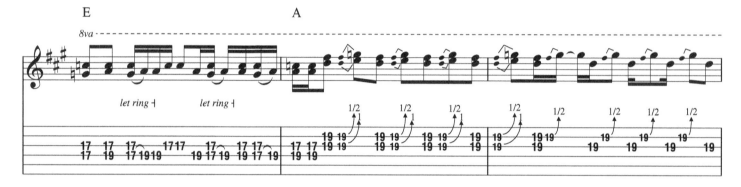

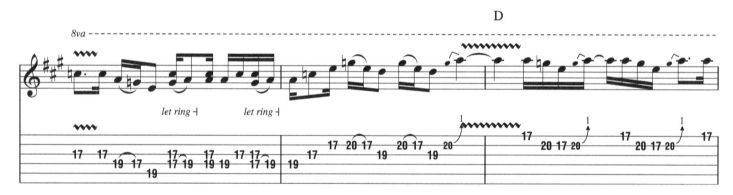

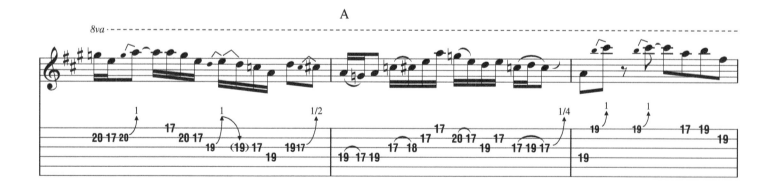

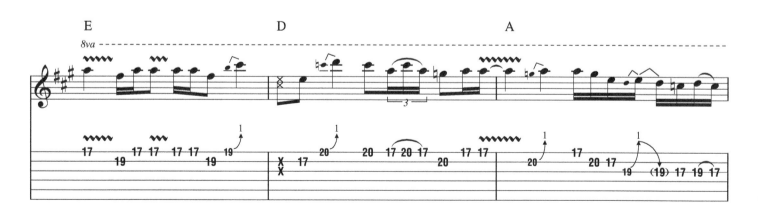

Outro-Verse

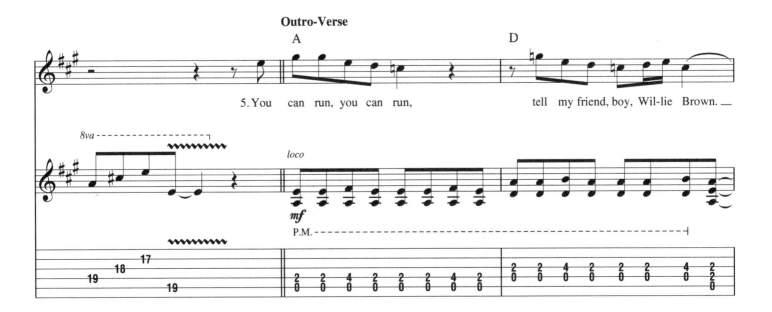

5. You can run, you can run, tell my friend, boy, Wil-lie Brown.

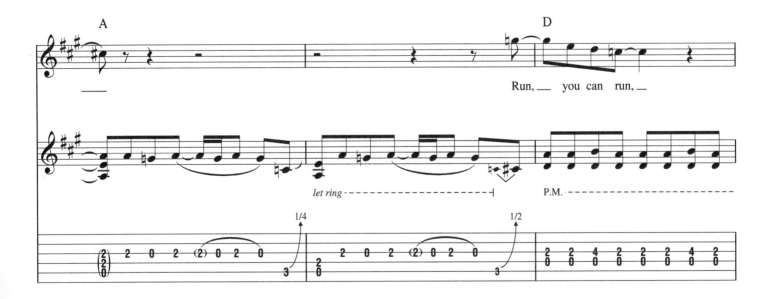

Run, you can run, tell my friend, boy, Wil-lie Brown.

tell my friend, boy, Wil-lie Brown. And I'm

stand-in' at the cross - road, be - lieve I'm__ sink - in' down.

Free time

Additional Lyrics

2. I went down to the crossroad, tried to flag a ride.
Down to the crossroad, tried to flag a ride.
Nobody seemed to know me. Ev'rybody passed me by.

3. When I'm goin' down to Rosedale, take my rider by my side.
Goin' down to Rosedale, take my rider by my side.
We can still barrelhouse, baby, on the riverside.

Sunshine of Your Love

Words and Music by Jack Bruce, Pete Brown and Eric Clapton

soon be with you, __ my __ love, __ to give you my dawn __ sur - prise. ____ I'll

be with you, dar - ling, soon. ____ I'll be with you when __ the stars __ start __ fall - ing.

To Coda ⊕

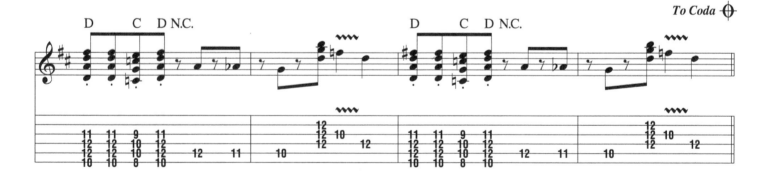

Chorus

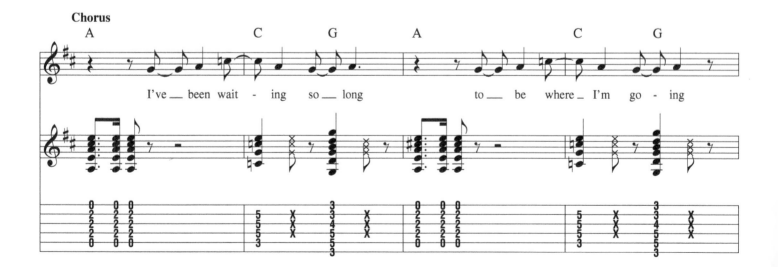

I've __ been wait - ing so __ long to __ be where __ I'm go - ing

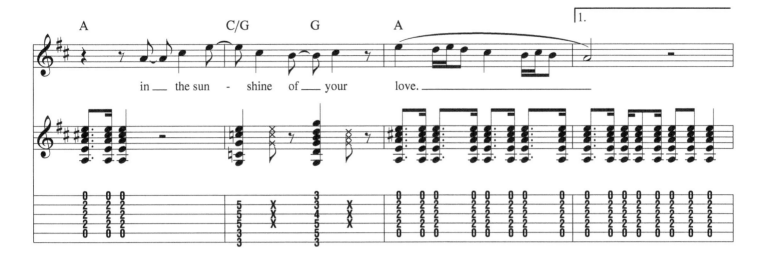

in ___ the sun - shine of ___ your love. ___

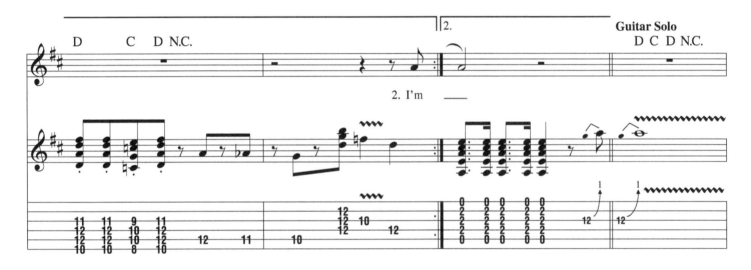

Guitar Solo

2. I'm ___

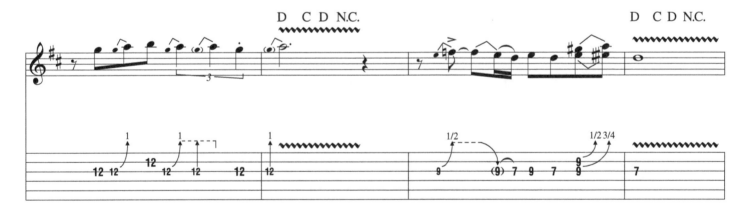

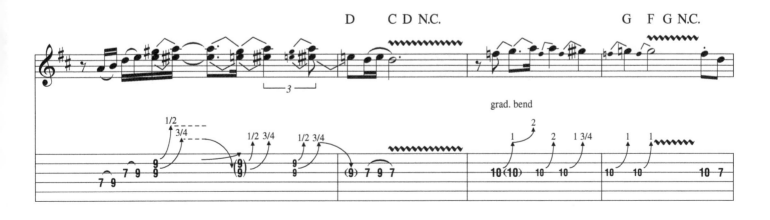

grad. bend

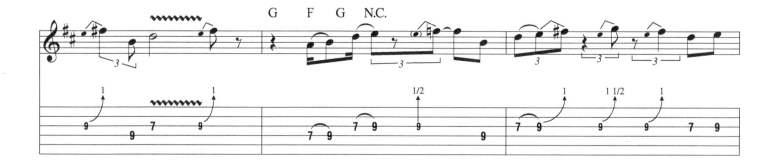

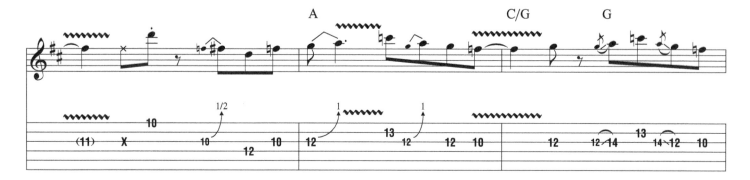

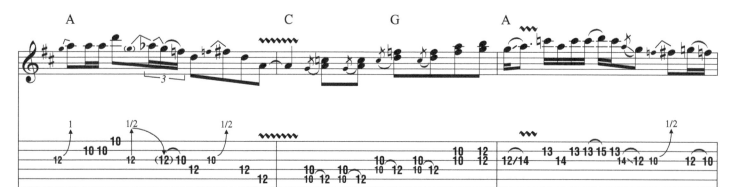

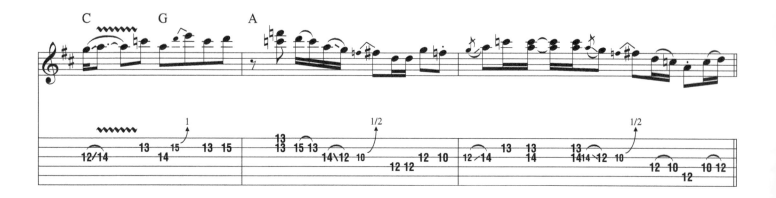

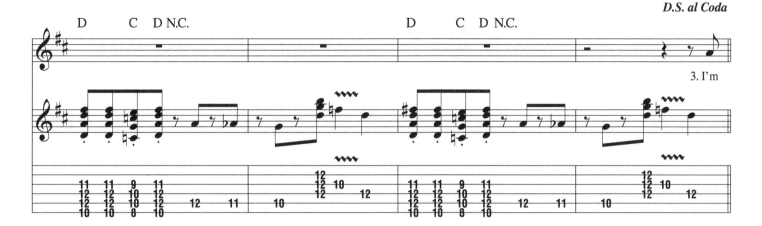

 Coda

Outro

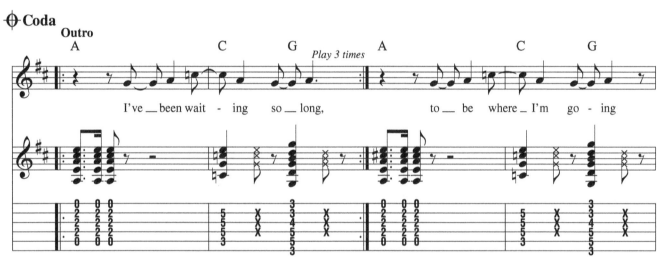

I've __ been wait - ing so __ long, to __ be where __ I'm go - ing

in __ the sun - shine of __ your love. _____

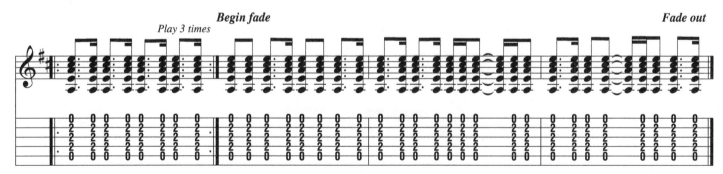

Additional Lyrics

I'm with you, my love;
The light shining through on you.
Yes, I'm with you, my love.
It's the morning and just we two.
I'll stay with you, darling, now.
I'll stay with you till my seeds are dried up.

Politician

Words and Music by Jack Bruce and Peter Brown

now, ba - by, uh, get in - to my big black car.

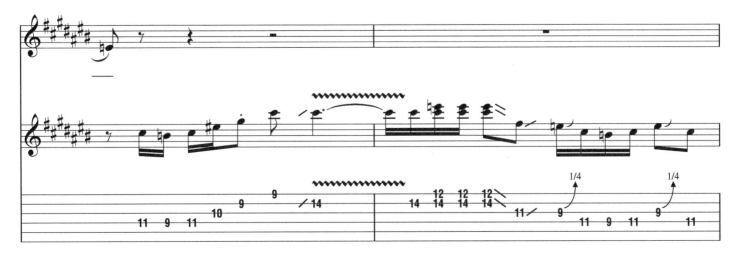

I wan - na just show you

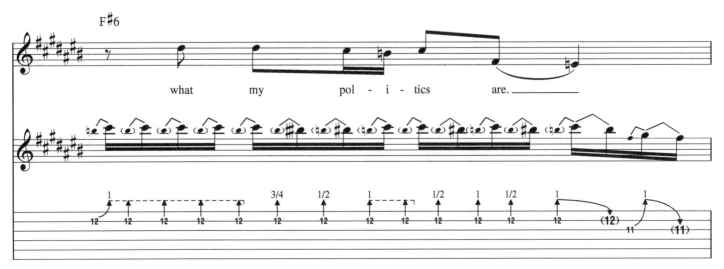

what my pol - i - tics are.

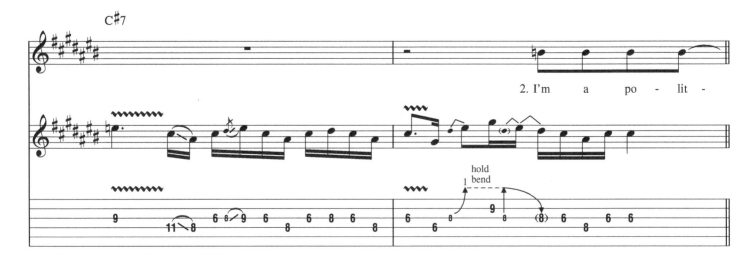

2. I'm a po - lit -

Verse

- i - cal man   and I prac - tice   what I ____   preach. ___

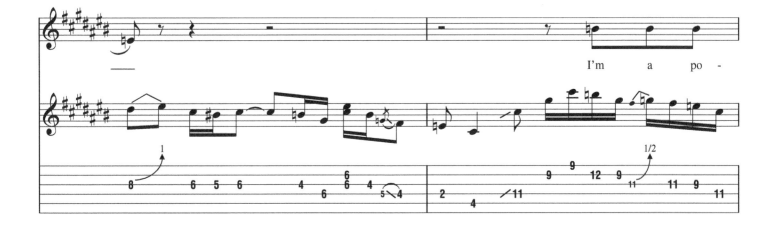

I'm a po -

lit - i - cal man ____   and I prac - tice   what I ____   preach. __

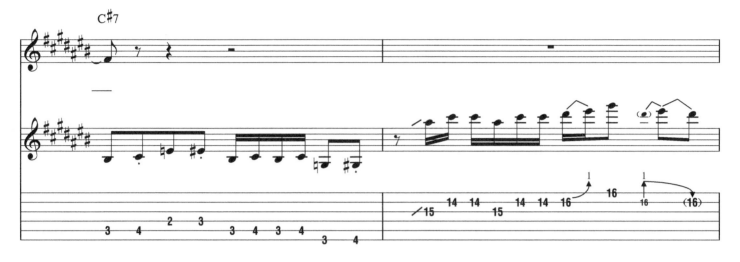

So don't de - ny __ me, ba - by, not while you're __ in my reach. __

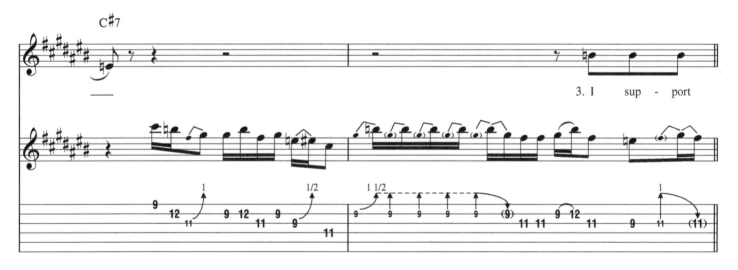

3. I sup - port

Verse

the left, __ though I'm __ lean - in', lean - in' to __ the

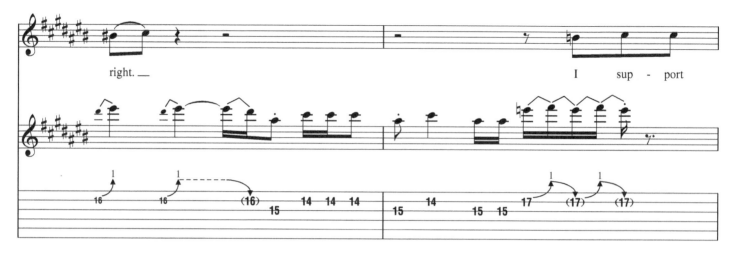

right. ___   I sup - port

F#7

the left ___   though I'm lean - in'   to ___ the ___

C#7

___ right. ___

let ring -|

G#6   F#6

But I'm just not there _____   when it's com - in' to   a   fight. ___

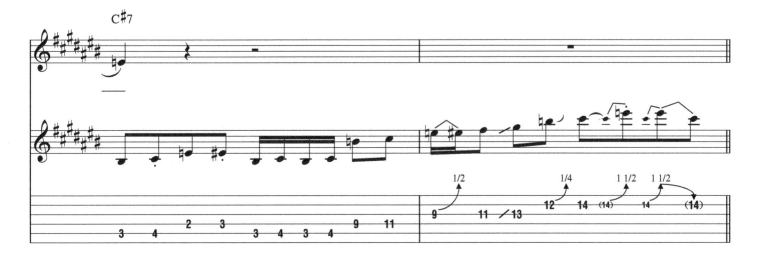

Guitar Solo

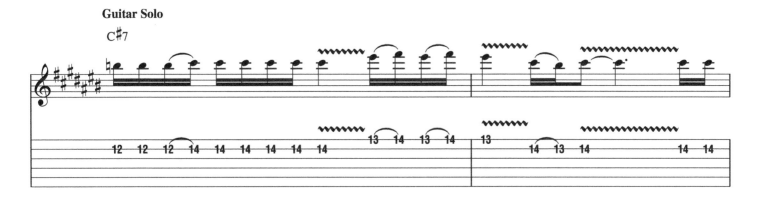

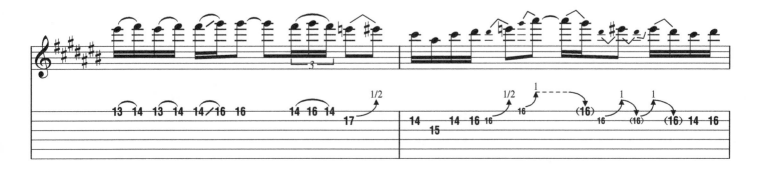

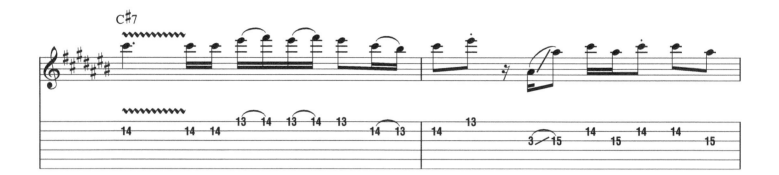

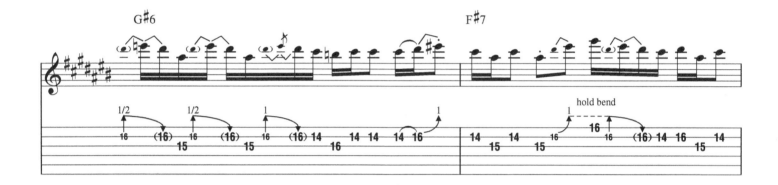

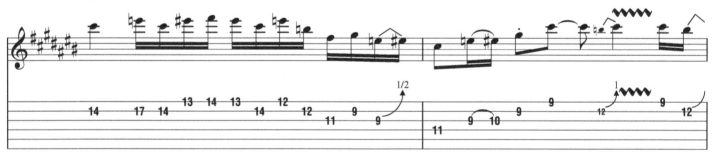

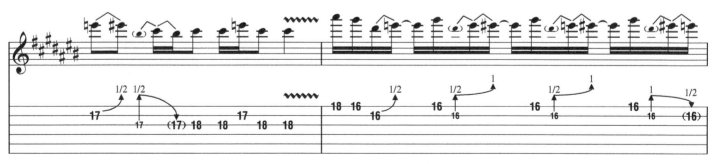

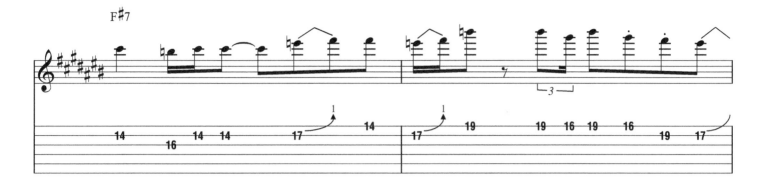

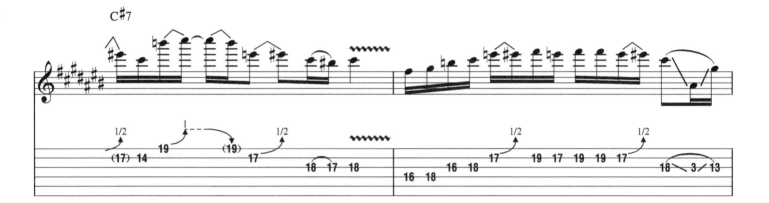

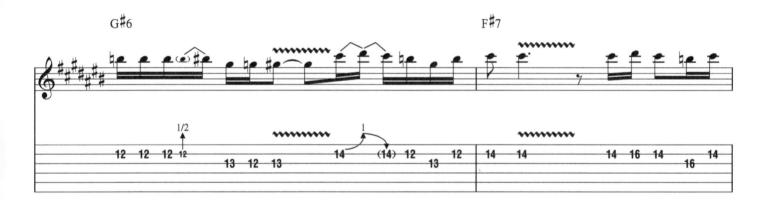

Verse

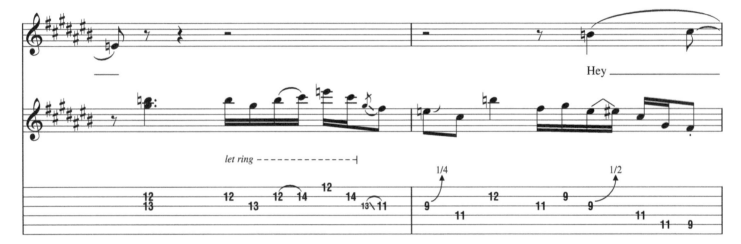

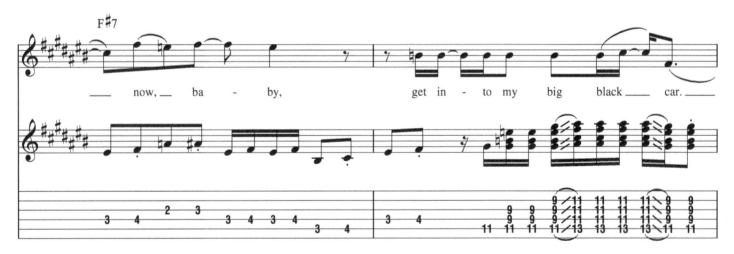

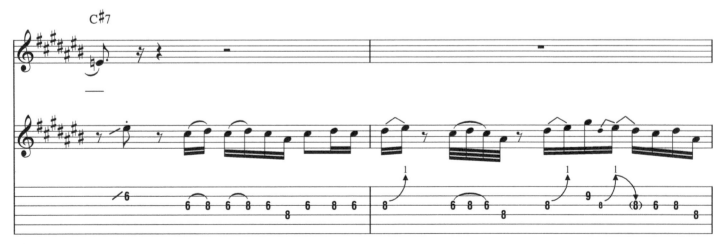

I wan - na just__ show you_____ what my__ pol - i - tics are. _____

Mm, _____

mm, _____ mm. _____

Begin fade

Fade out

Spoonful

Words and Music by Willie Dixon

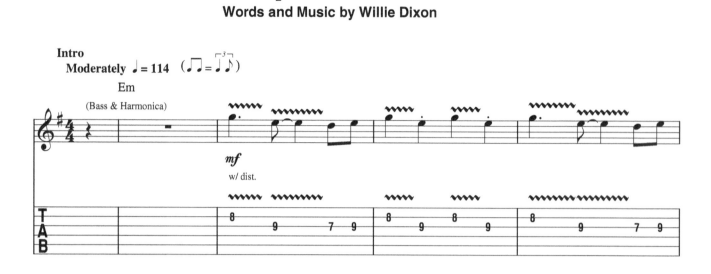

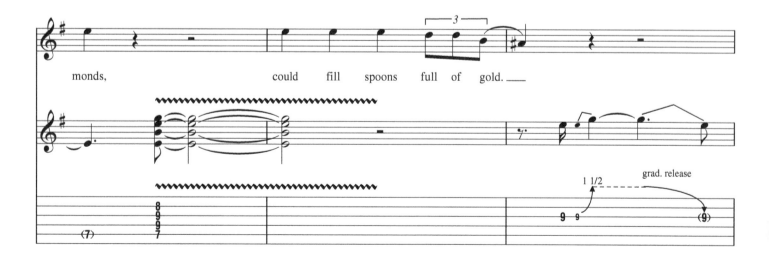

spoon, that spoon, that spoon - ful. ____ That spoon, that spoon, that

spoon - ful. ____ That spoon, that spoon, that spoon - ful. ____ That

Harmonica Solo

Em

spoon, that spoon, that spoon.

36

Verse

2. Could fill spoons full of cof - fee,

could fill spoons full of tea. _____ Just a _____ lit - tle spoon of your _____

pre - cious love, _____ is that _____ e - nough _ for _ me? _ Men _____

spoon, that spoon, that spoon - ful.___ That spoon, that spoon, hey._____

Guitar Solo

Em

*Played behind the beat.

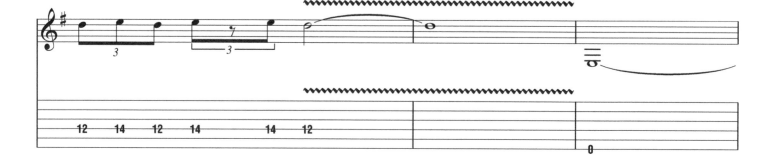

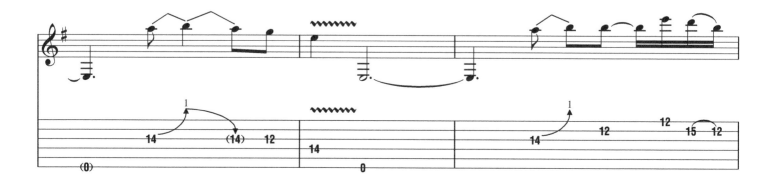

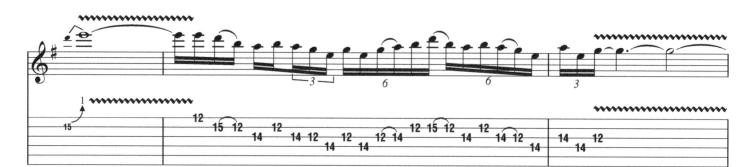

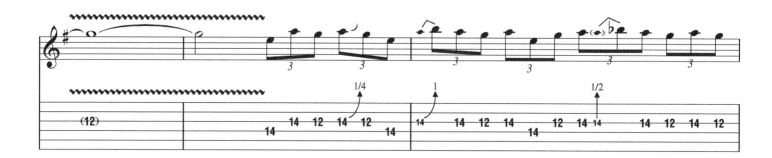

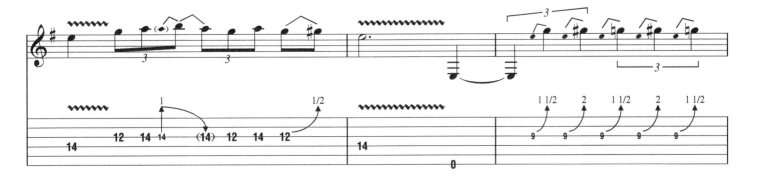

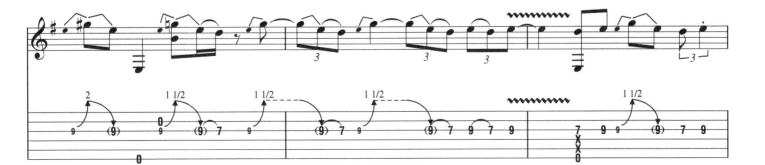

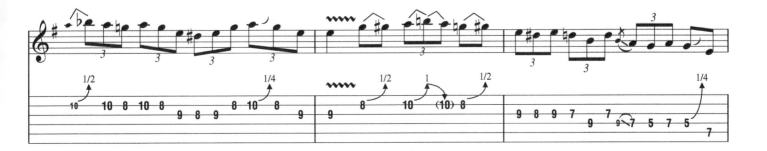

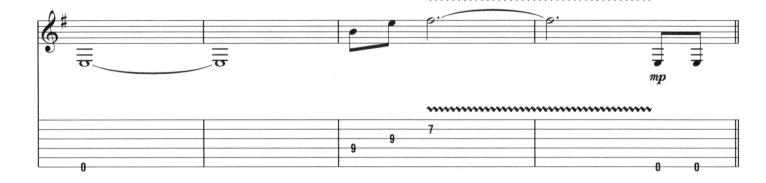

Interlude

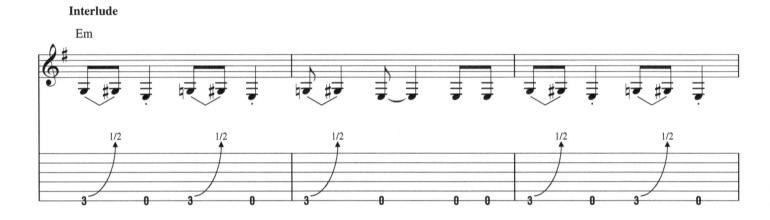

Verse

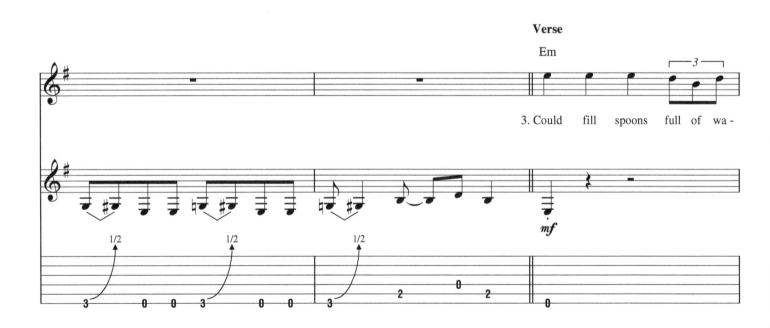

3. Could fill spoons full of wa-

ter, _____ saved them from the des - ert sands. _____

Was a lit - tle spoon of your love, ba - by, _____ saved you from an - oth - er man. _

Men lies _____ a, some of them _

_ cries _____ a - bout _ it, _ some of them dies. _____

spoon - ful, ___ spoon - ful. _____

Hey! _____

Ev - 'ry - thing's _ dy - in' a - bout it, ___ yeah. Al - right, just

cry - in' a - bout it. ___ That spoon, that spoon, that

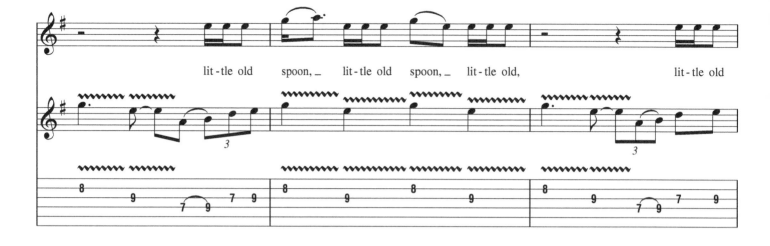

lit-tle old spoon,__ lit-tle old spoon,__ lit-tle old, lit-tle old

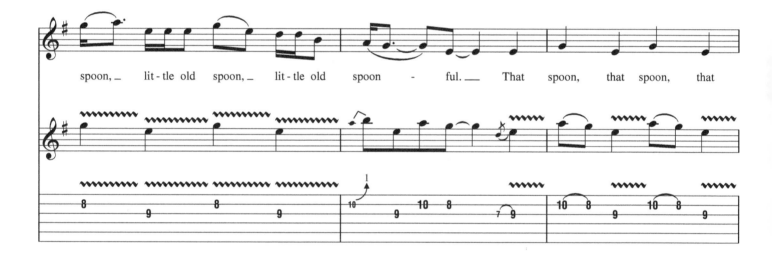

spoon,__ lit-tle old spoon,__ lit-tle old spoon - ful.__ That spoon, that spoon, that

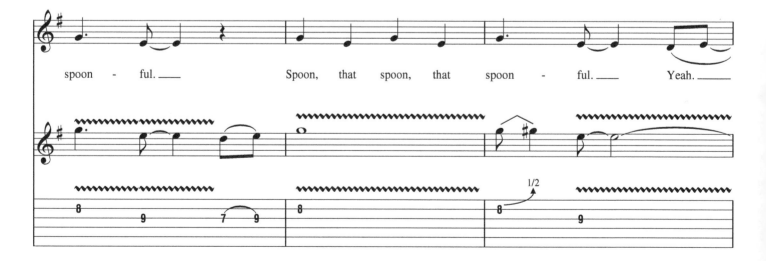

spoon - ful.___ Spoon, that spoon, that spoon - ful.___ Yeah.___

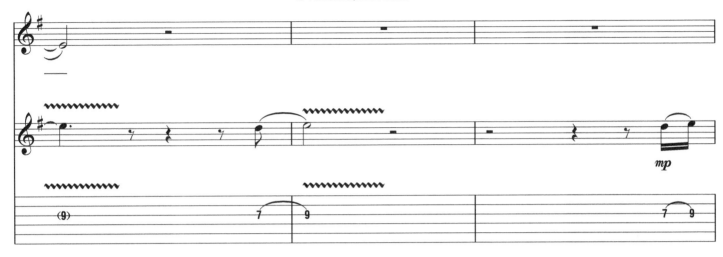

Outro
Free time

N.C.

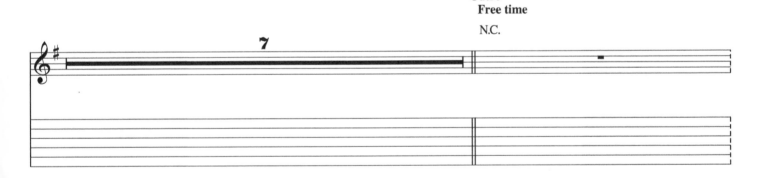

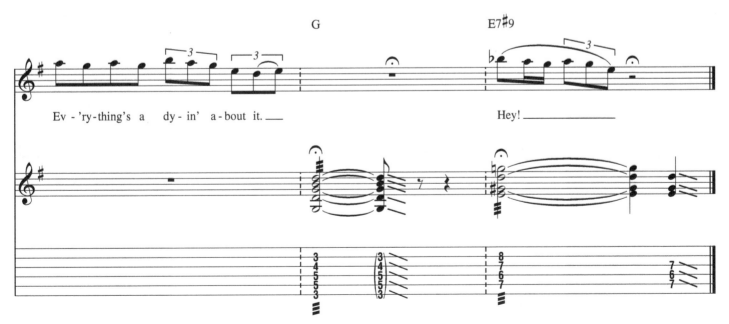

Ev -'ry-thing's a   dy - in' a-bout it. ___   Hey! _____

Strange Brew

Words and Music by Eric Clapton, Felix Pappalardi and Gail Collins

Intro
Moderately ♩ = 108

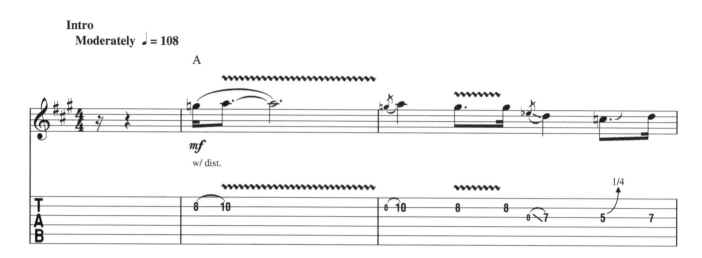

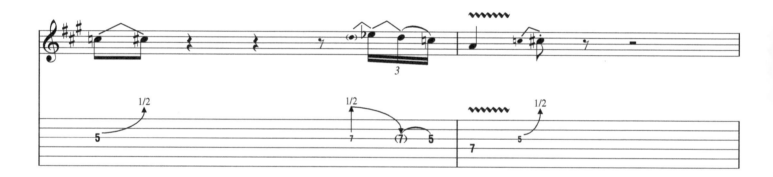

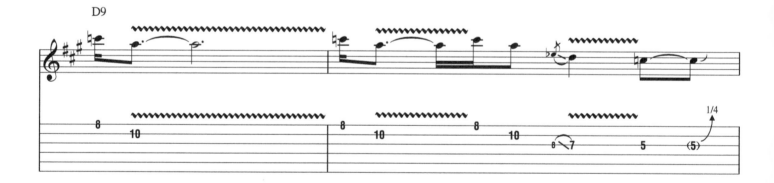

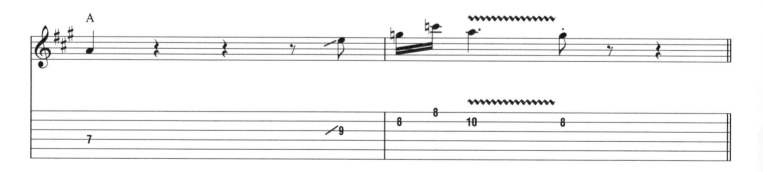

Chorus

Strange _____ brew kill - in' what's in - side _____ of you. _____

1. She's a

Verse

witch of _____ trou - ble in e - lec - tric blue. _____ In her

own mad mind she's in love with you, with you. _____

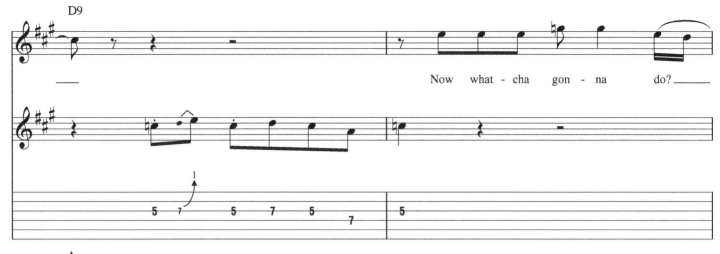

Now what-cha gon-na do?

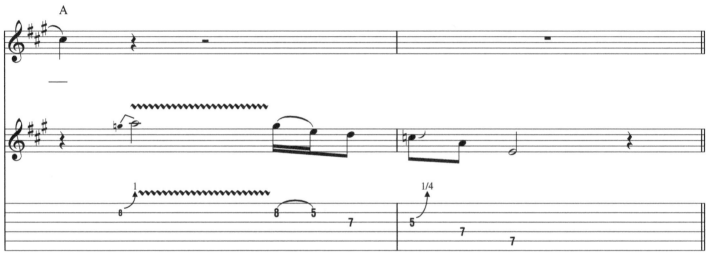

Chorus

Strange _____ brew kill - in' what's in - side _____ of you. _____

2. She's

50

Verse

some kind-a de-mon dash-in'___ in the___ blue.___ If you

don't watch out,___ it-'ll stick to you, to you.___

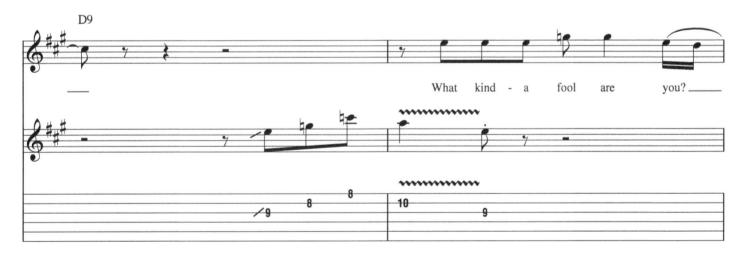

What kind-a fool are you?___

Chorus

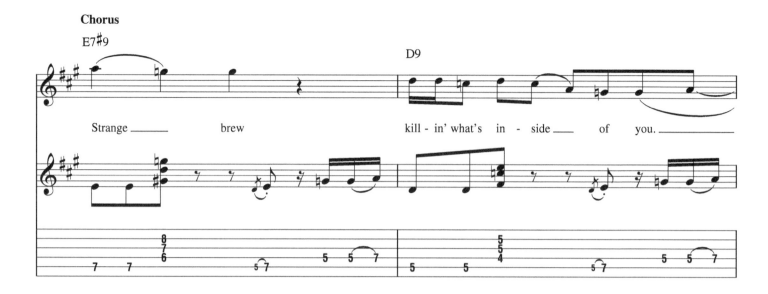

Strange _____ brew _____ kill - in' what's in - side _____ of you. _____

Guitar Solo

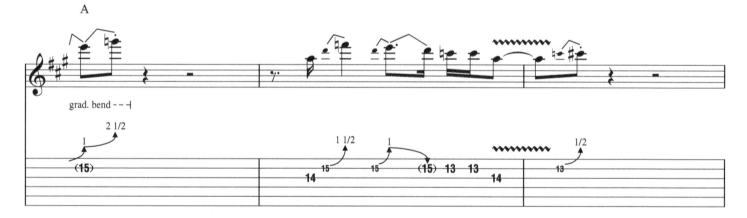

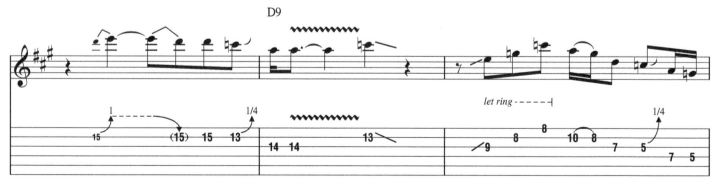

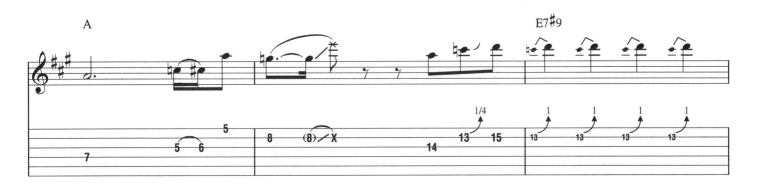

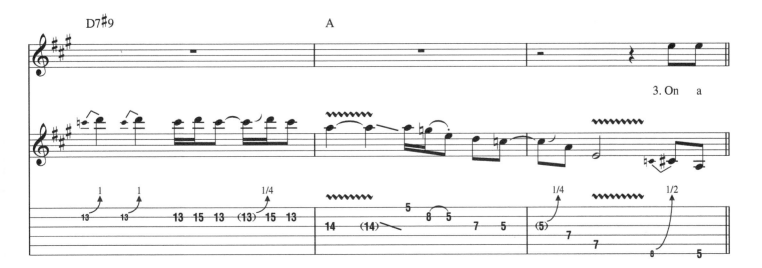

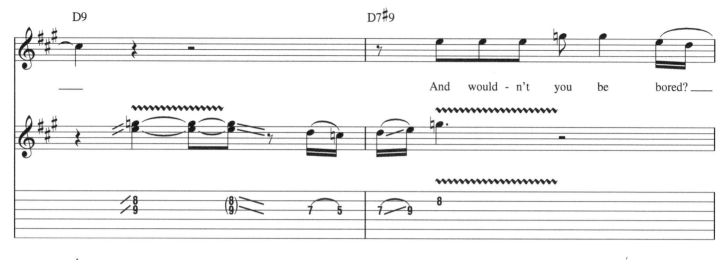

And would - n't you be bored? ___

Chorus

Strange ___ brew kill - in' what's in - side ___ of you. ___

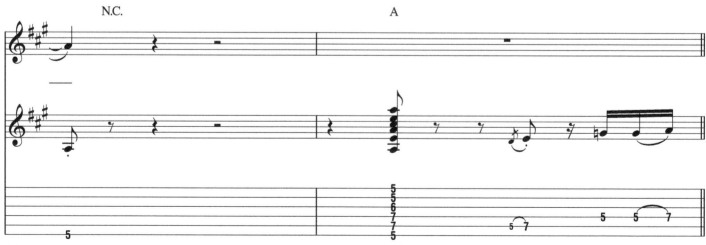

Tales of Brave Ulysses

Words and Music by Eric Clapton and Martin Sharp

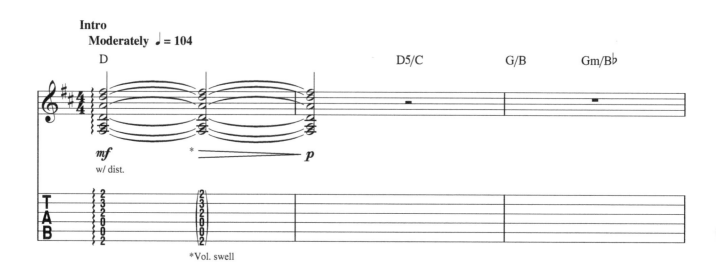

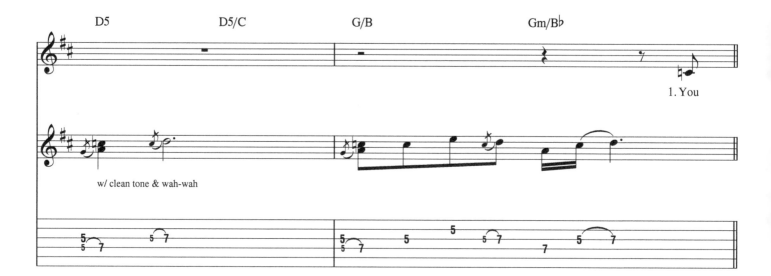

Interlude

2. And the

mf

w/ wah-wah

Verse

col - ors of the sea ___ blind your eyes with trem - bling mer - maids and you

3. *See additional lyrics.*

touch the dis - tant beach - es with tales of brave U - lys - ses, how his

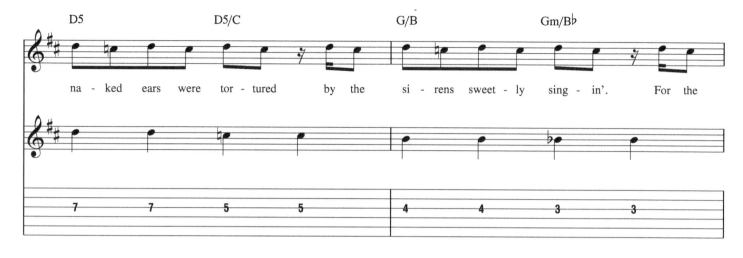

na - ked ears were tor - tured by the si - rens sweet - ly sing - in'. For the

spar - kling waves are call - ing you to kiss their white - laced ___ lips.

1.

Guitar Solo

w/ dist. & wah-wah

3. And you

Guitar Solo

Verse

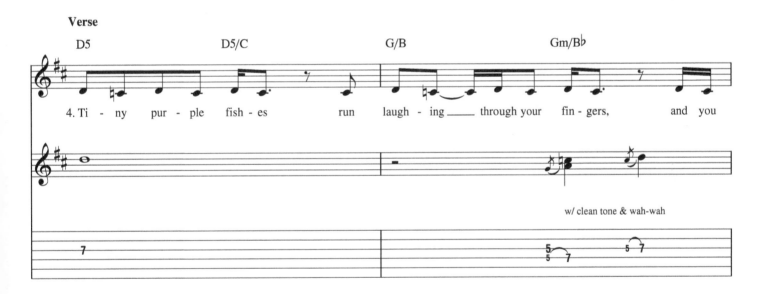

4. Ti - ny pur - ple fish - es run laugh - ing ___ through your fin - gers, and you

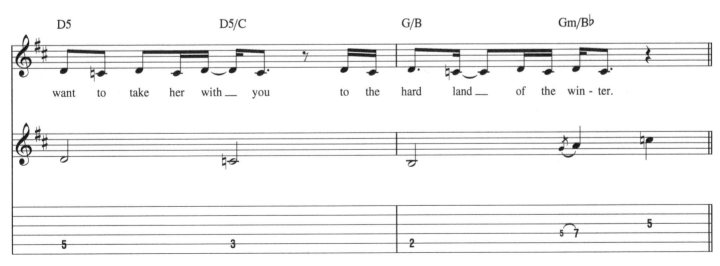

want to take her with ___ you to the hard land ___ of the win - ter.

Interlude

Verse

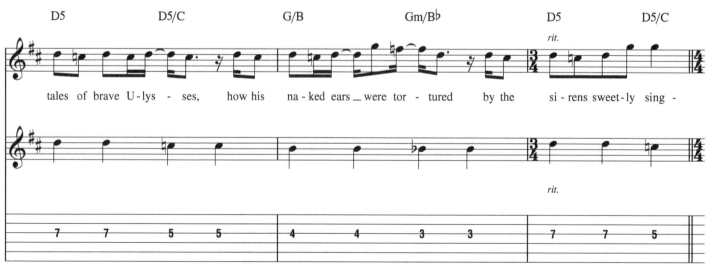

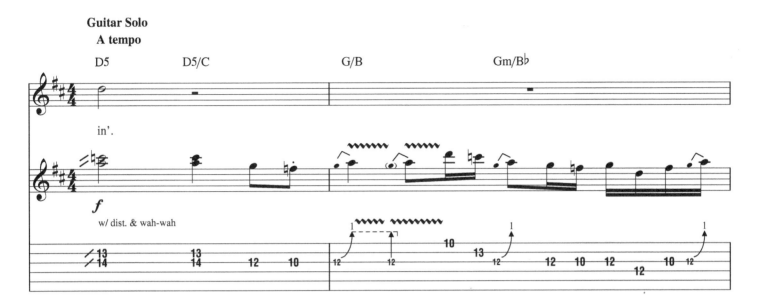

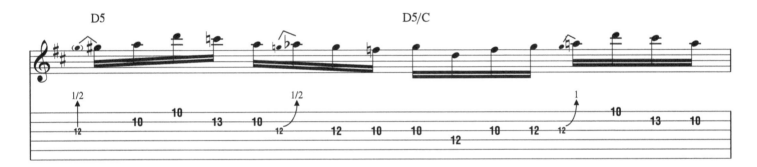

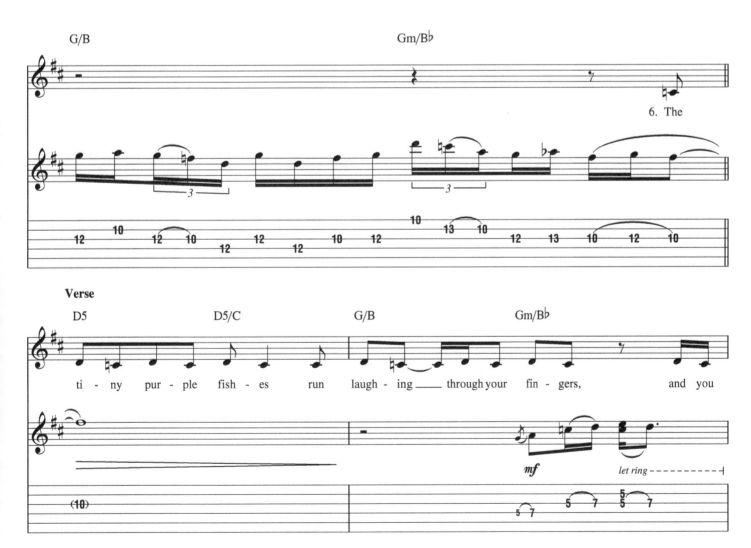

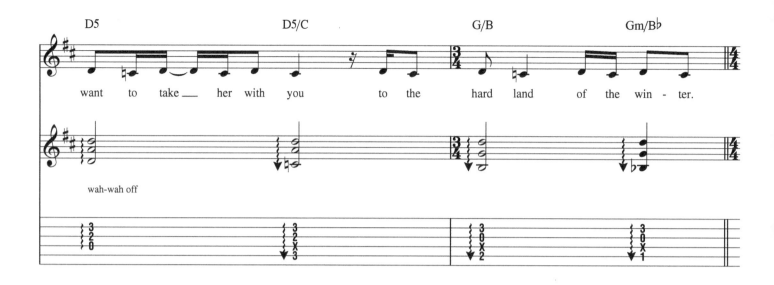

want   to   take ___   her   with   you   to   the   hard   land   of   the   win - ter.

wah-wah off

Outro-Guitar Solo

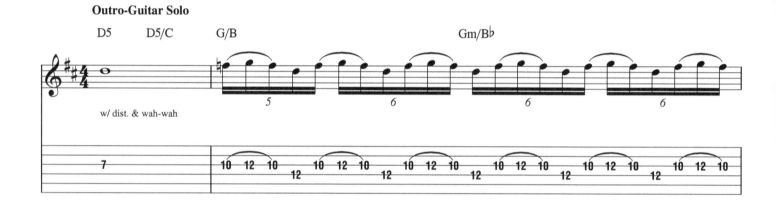

w/ dist. & wah-wah

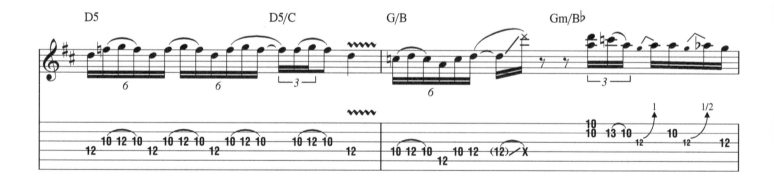

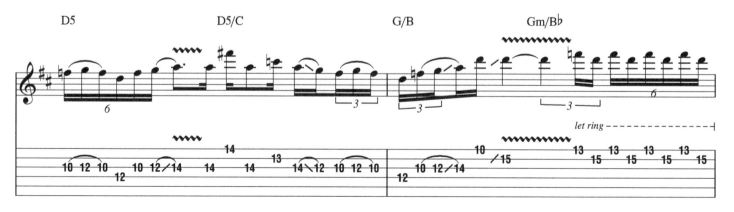

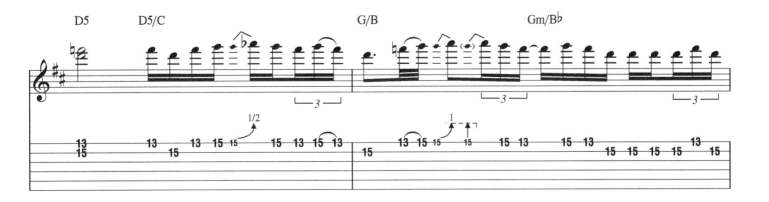

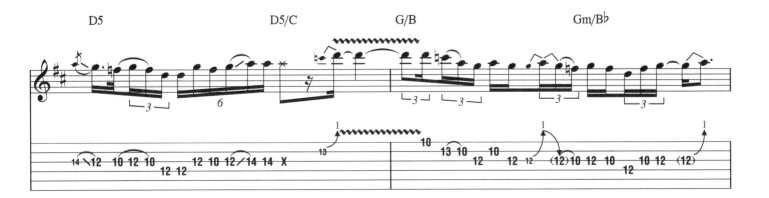

Begin fade

Fade out

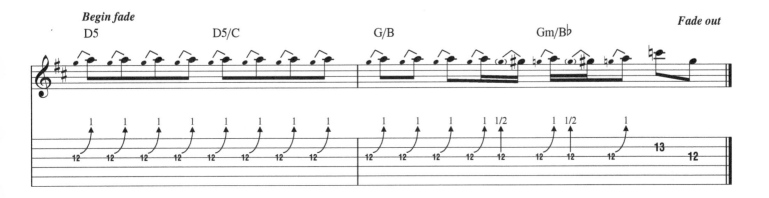

Additional Lyrics

3. And you see your girl's brown body
   Dancing through the turquoise
   And her footprints make you follow
   Where the sky loves the sea.
   And when your fingers find her,
   She drowns you in her body.
   Carving deep blue ripples
   In the tissues of your mind.

White Room

Words and Music by Jack Bruce and Pete Brown

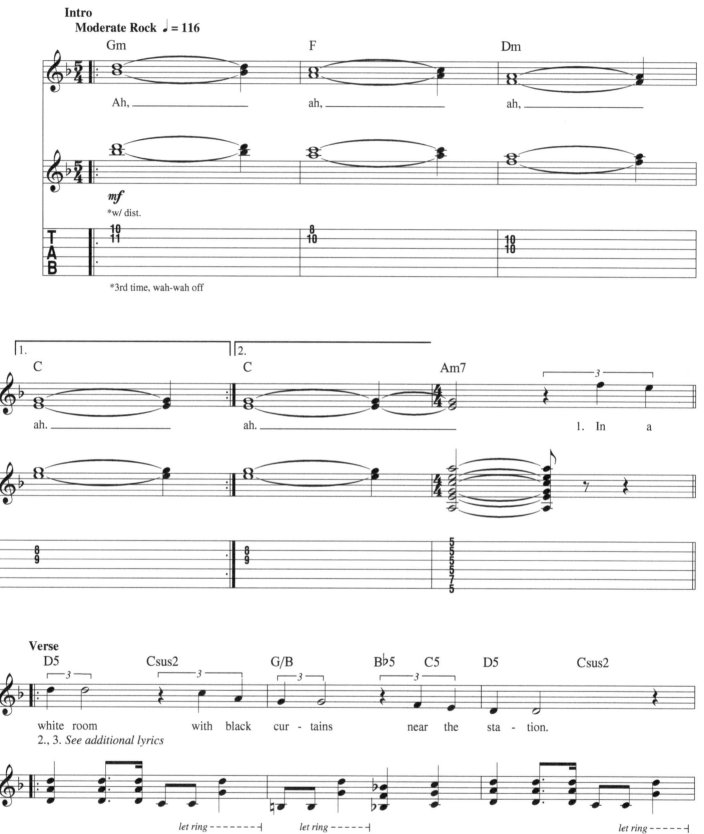

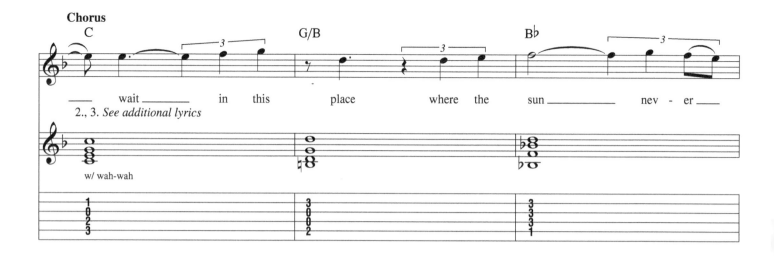

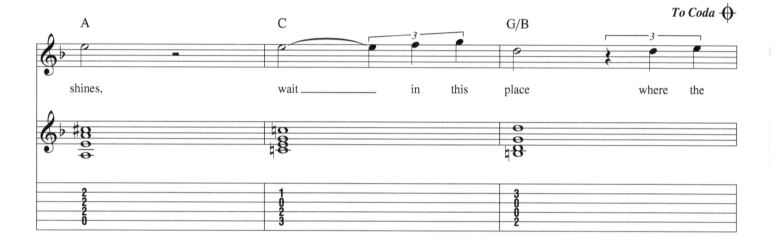

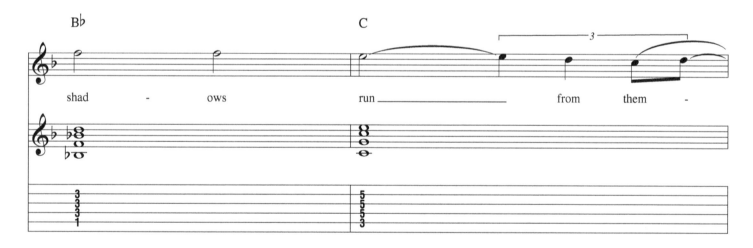

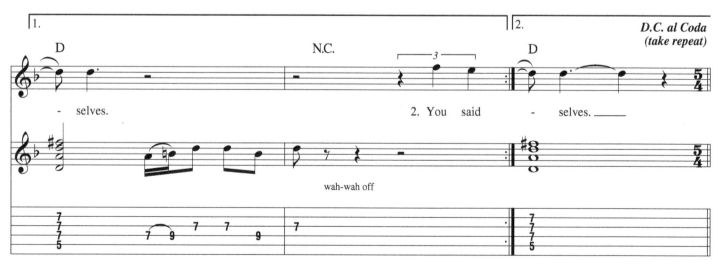

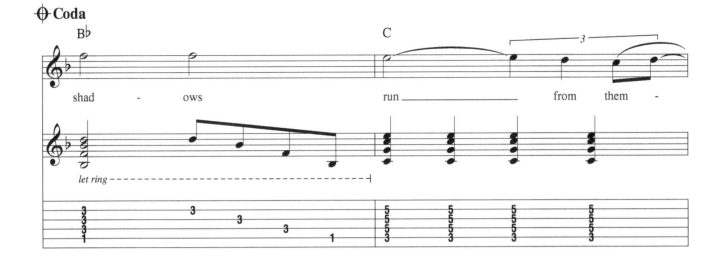

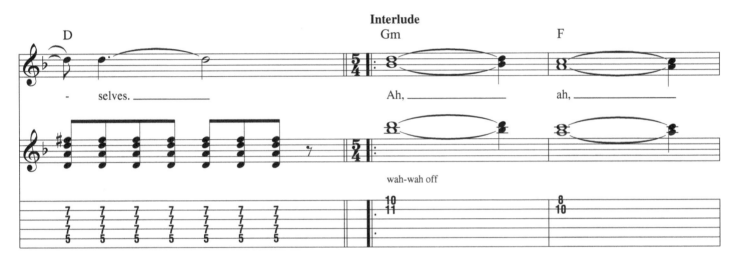

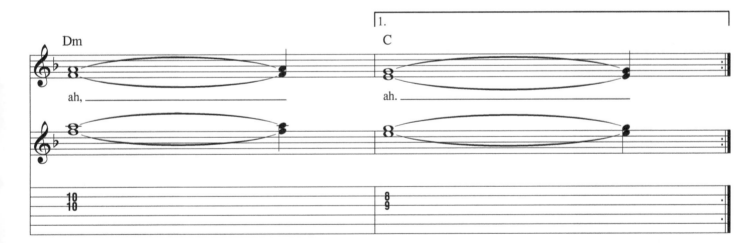

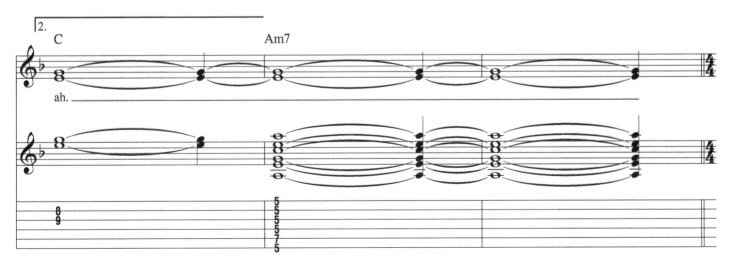

Outro-Guitar Solo

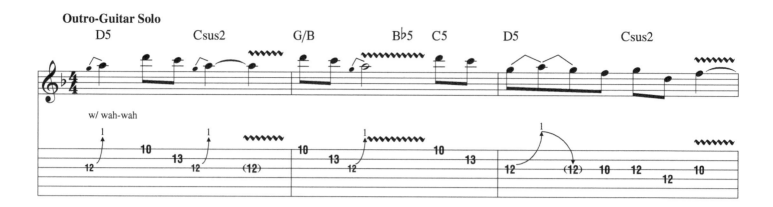

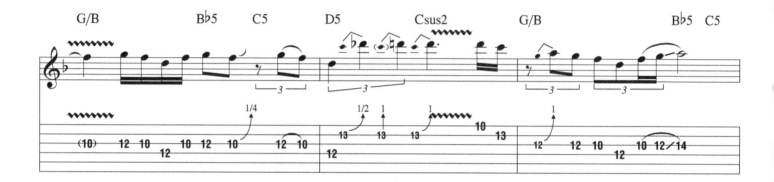

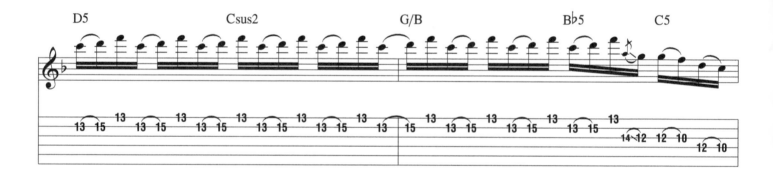

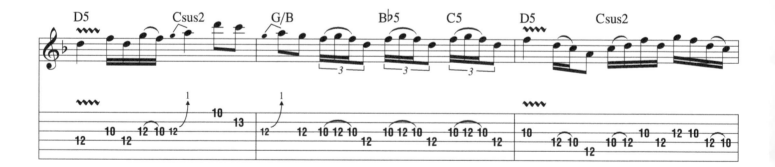

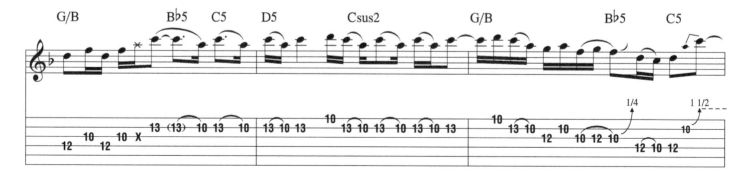

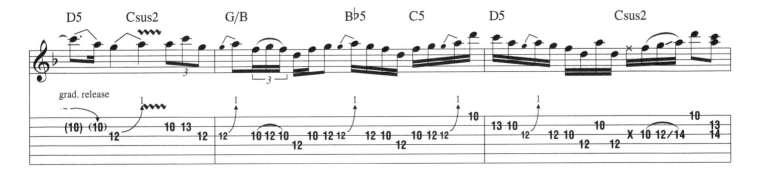

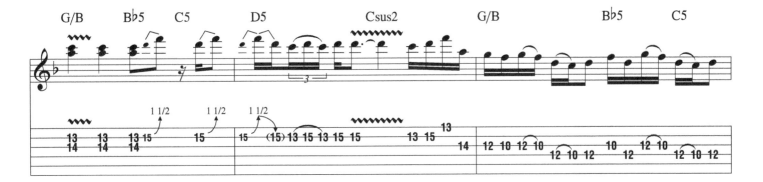

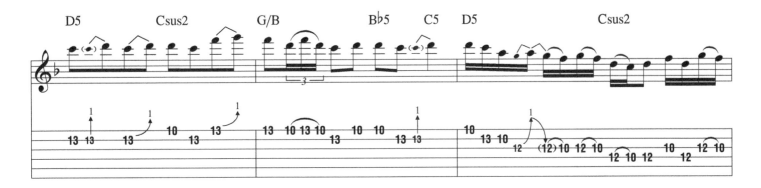

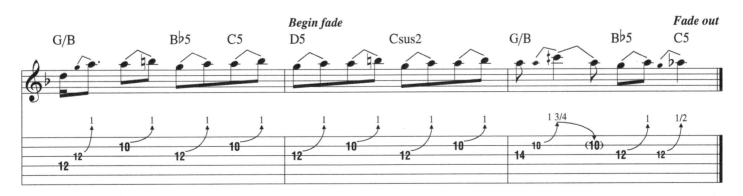

Additional Lyrics

2. You said no strings could secure you at the station.
   Platform ticket, restless diesel, goodbye windows.
   I walked into such a sad time at the station.
   As I walked out felt my own need just beginning.

Chorus 2. I'll wait in the queue when the trains come back.
   Lie with you where the shadows run from themselves.

3. At the party she was kindness in the hard crowd.
   Isolation for the old queen now forgotten.
   Yellow tigers crouched in jungles in her dark eyes.
   She's just dressing goodbye windows, tired starling.

Chorus 3. I'll sleep in this place with the lonely crowd.
   Lie in the dark, where the shadows run from themselves.

HAL•LEONARD GUITAR PLAY-ALONG

INCLUDES TAB
AUDIO ACCESS INCLUDED

This series will help you play your favorite songs quickly and easily. Just follow the tab and listen to the audio to hear how the guitar should sound, and then play along using the separate backing tracks.

Playback tools are provided for slowing down the tempo without changing pitch and looping challenging parts. The melody and lyrics are included in the book so that you can sing or simply follow along.

1. ROCK
00699570.................$17.99

2. ACOUSTIC
00699569.................$16.99

3. HARD ROCK
00699573.................$17.99

4. POP/ROCK
00699571.................$16.99

5. THREE CHORD SONGS
00300985.................$16.99

6. '90S ROCK
00298615.................$16.99

7. BLUES
00699575.................$19.99

8. ROCK
00699585.................$16.99

9. EASY ACOUSTIC SONGS
00151708.................$16.99

10. ACOUSTIC
00699586.................$16.95

11. EARLY ROCK
00699579.................$15.99

12. ROCK POP
00291724.................$16.99

14. BLUES ROCK
00699582.................$16.99

15. R&B
00699583.................$17.99

16. JAZZ
00699584.................$16.99

17. COUNTRY
00699588.................$17.99

18. ACOUSTIC ROCK
00699577.................$15.95

20. ROCKABILLY
00699580.................$17.99

21. SANTANA
00174525.................$17.99

22. CHRISTMAS
00699600.................$15.99

23. SURF
00699635.................$17.99

24. ERIC CLAPTON
00699649.................$19.99

25. THE BEATLES
00198265.................$19.99

26. ELVIS PRESLEY
00699643.................$16.99

27. DAVID LEE ROTH
00699645.................$16.95

28. GREG KOCH
00699646.................$19.99

29. BOB SEGER
00699647.................$16.99

30. KISS
00699644.................$17.99

32. THE OFFSPRING
00699653.................$14.95

33. ACOUSTIC CLASSICS
00699656.................$19.99

34. CLASSIC ROCK
00699658.................$17.99

35. HAIR METAL
00699660.................$17.99

36. SOUTHERN ROCK
00699661.................$19.99

37. ACOUSTIC UNPLUGGED
00699662.................$22.99

38. BLUES
00699663.................$17.99

39. '80S METAL
00699664.................$17.99

40. INCUBUS
00699668.................$17.95

41. ERIC CLAPTON
00699669.................$17.99

42. COVER BAND HITS
00211597.................$16.99

43. LYNYRD SKYNYRD
00699681.................$22.99

44. JAZZ GREATS
00699689.................$16.99

45. TV THEMES
00699718.................$14.95

46. MAINSTREAM ROCK
00699722.................$16.95

47. HENDRIX SMASH HITS
00699723.................$19.99

48. AEROSMITH CLASSICS
00699724.................$17.99

49. STEVIE RAY VAUGHAN
00699725.................$17.99

50. VAN HALEN 1978-1984
00110269.................$19.99

51. ALTERNATIVE '90S
00699727.................$14.99

52. FUNK
00699728.................$15.99

53. DISCO
00699729.................$14.99

54. HEAVY METAL
00699730.................$17.99

55. POP METAL
00699731.................$14.95

57. GUNS N' ROSES
00159922.................$17.99

58. BLINK-182
00699772.................$14.95

59. CHET ATKINS
00702347.................$17.99

60. 3 DOORS DOWN
00699774.................$14.95

62. CHRISTMAS CAROLS
00699798.................$12.95

63. CREEDENCE CLEARWATER REVIVAL
00699802.................$17.99

64. OZZY OSBOURNE
00699803.................$19.99

66. THE ROLLING STONES
00699807.................$19.99

67. BLACK SABBATH
00699808.................$17.99

68. PINK FLOYD – DARK SIDE OF THE MOON
00699809.................$17.99

71. CHRISTIAN ROCK
00699824.................$14.95

72. ACOUSTIC '90S
00699827.................$14.95

73. BLUESY ROCK
00699829.................$17.99

74. SIMPLE STRUMMING SONGS
00151706.................$19.99

75. TOM PETTY
00699882.................$19.99

76. COUNTRY HITS
00699884.................$16.99

77. BLUEGRASS
00699910.................$17.99

78. NIRVANA
00700132.................$17.99

79. NEIL YOUNG
00700133.................$24.99

81. ROCK ANTHOLOGY
00700176.................$22.99

82. EASY ROCK SONGS
00700177.................$17.99

84. STEELY DAN
00700200.................$19.99

85. THE POLICE
00700269.................$16.99

86. BOSTON
00700465.................$19.99

87. ACOUSTIC WOMEN
00700763.................$14.99

88. GRUNGE
00700467.................$16.99

89. REGGAE
00700468.................$15.99

90. CLASSICAL POP
00700469.................$14.99

91. BLUES INSTRUMENTALS
00700505.................$19.99

92. EARLY ROCK INSTRUMENTALS
00700506.................$17.99

93. ROCK INSTRUMENTALS
00700507.................$17.99

94. SLOW BLUES
00700508.................$16.99

95. BLUES CLASSICS
00700509.................$15.99

96. BEST COUNTRY HITS
00211615.................$16.99

97. CHRISTMAS CLASSICS
00236542.................$14.99

98. ROCK BAND
00700704.................$14.95

99. ZZ TOP
00700762.................$16.99

100. B.B. KING
00700466.................$16.99

101. SONGS FOR BEGINNERS
00701917.................$14.99

102. CLASSIC PUNK
00700769.................$14.99

104. DUANE ALLMAN
00700846.................$22.99

105. LATIN
00700939.................$16.99

106. WEEZER
00700958.................$17.99

107. CREAM
00701069............$17.99

108. THE WHO
00701053............$17.99

109. STEVE MILLER
00701054............$19.99

110. SLIDE GUITAR HITS
00701055............$17.99

111. JOHN MELLENCAMP
00701056............$14.99

112. QUEEN
00701052............$16.99

113. JIM CROCE
00701058............$19.99

114. BON JOVI
00701060............$17.99

115. JOHNNY CASH
00701070............$17.99

116. THE VENTURES
00701124............$17.99

117. BRAD PAISLEY
00701224............$16.99

118. ERIC JOHNSON
00701353............$17.99

119. AC/DC CLASSICS
00701356............$19.99

120. PROGRESSIVE ROCK
00701457............$14.99

121. U2
00701508............$17.99

122. CROSBY, STILLS & NASH
00701610............$16.99

123. LENNON & McCARTNEY ACOUSTIC
00701614............$16.99

124. SMOOTH JAZZ
00200664............$16.99

125. JEFF BECK
00701687............$19.99

126. BOB MARLEY
00701701............$17.99

127. 1970S ROCK
00701739............$17.99

128. 1960S ROCK
00701740............$14.99

129. MEGADETH
00701741............$17.99

130. IRON MAIDEN
00701742............$17.99

131. 1990S ROCK
00701743............$14.99

132. COUNTRY ROCK
00701757............$15.99

133. TAYLOR SWIFT
00701894............$16.99

135. MINOR BLUES
00151350............$17.99

136. GUITAR THEMES
00701922............$14.99

137. IRISH TUNES
00701966............$15.99

138. BLUEGRASS CLASSICS
00701967............$17.99

139. GARY MOORE
00702370............$17.99

140. MORE STEVIE RAY VAUGHAN
00702396............$19.99

141. ACOUSTIC HITS
00702401............$16.99

142. GEORGE HARRISON
00237697............$17.99

143. SLASH
00702425............$19.99

144. DJANGO REINHARDT
00702531............$17.99

145. DEF LEPPARD
00702532............$19.99

146. ROBERT JOHNSON
00702533............$16.99

147. SIMON & GARFUNKEL
14041591............$17.99

148. BOB DYLAN
14041592............$17.99

149. AC/DC HITS
14041593............$19.99

150. ZAKK WYLDE
02501717............$19.99

151. J.S. BACH
02501730............$16.99

152. JOE BONAMASSA
02501751............$24.99

153. RED HOT CHILI PEPPERS
00702990............$22.99

155. ERIC CLAPTON – FROM THE ALBUM UNPLUGGED
00703085 ....$17.99

156. SLAYER
00703770............$19.99

157. FLEETWOOD MAC
00101382............$17.99

159. WES MONTGOMERY
00102593............$22.99

160. T-BONE WALKER
00102641............$17.99

161. THE EAGLES – ACOUSTIC
00102659............$19.99

162. THE EAGLES HITS
00102667............$17.99

163. PANTERA
00103036............$19.99

164. VAN HALEN 1986-1995
00110270............$19.99

165. GREEN DAY
00210343............$17.99

166. MODERN BLUES
00700764............$16.99

167. DREAM THEATER
00111938............$24.99

168. KISS
00113421............$17.99

169. TAYLOR SWIFT
00115982............$16.99

170. THREE DAYS GRACE
00117337............$16.99

171. JAMES BROWN
00117420............$16.99

172. THE DOOBIE BROTHERS
00119670............$17.99

173. TRANS-SIBERIAN ORCHESTRA
00119907............$19.99

174. SCORPIONS
00122119............$19.99

175. MICHAEL SCHENKER
00122127............$17.99

176. BLUES BREAKERS WITH JOHN MAYALL & ERIC CLAPTON
00122132............$19.99

177. ALBERT KING
00123271............$17.99

178. JASON MRAZ
00124165............$17.99

179. RAMONES
00127073............$16.99

180. BRUNO MARS
00129706............$16.99

181. JACK JOHNSON
00129854............$16.99

182. SOUNDGARDEN
00138161............$17.99

183. BUDDY GUY
00138240............$17.99

184. KENNY WAYNE SHEPHERD
00138258............$17.99

185. JOE SATRIANI
00139457............$19.99

186. GRATEFUL DEAD
00139459............$17.99

187. JOHN DENVER
00140839............$19.99

188. MÖTLEY CRUE
00141145............$19.99

189. JOHN MAYER
00144350............$19.99

190. DEEP PURPLE
00146152............$19.99

191. PINK FLOYD CLASSICS
00146164............$17.99

192. JUDAS PRIEST
00151352............$19.99

193. STEVE VAI
00156028............$19.99

194. PEARL JAM
00157925............$17.99

195. METALLICA: 1983-1988
00234291............$22.99

196. METALLICA: 1991-2016
00234292............$19.99

HAL•LEONARD®

For complete songlists, visit
Hal Leonard online at
www.halleonard.com

Prices, contents, and availability subject to
change without notice.

RECORDED VERSIONS®
The Best Note-For-Note Transcriptions Available

**AUTHENTIC TRANSCRIPTIONS
WITH NOTES AND TABLATURE**

00690603	Aerosmith – O Yeah! Ultimate Hits	$29.99
00690178	Alice in Chains – Acoustic	$22.99
00694865	Alice in Chains – Dirt	$19.99
00694925	Alice in Chains – Jar of Flies/Sap	$19.99
00691091	Alice Cooper – Best of	$24.99
00690958	Duane Allman – Guitar Anthology	$29.99
00694932	Allman Brothers Band – Volume 1	$29.99
00694933	Allman Brothers Band – Volume 2	$27.99
00694934	Allman Brothers Band – Volume 3	$29.99
00690945	Alter Bridge – Blackbird	$24.99
00123558	Arctic Monkeys – AM	$24.99
00214869	Avenged Sevenfold – Best of 2005-2013	$24.99
00690489	Beatles – 1	$24.99
00694929	Beatles – 1962-1966	$27.99
00694930	Beatles – 1967-1970	$29.99
00694880	Beatles – Abbey Road	$19.99
00694832	Beatles – Acoustic Guitar	$27.99
00690110	Beatles – White Album (Book 1)	$19.99
00692385	Chuck Berry	$24.99
00147787	Black Crowes – Best of	$24.99
00690149	Black Sabbath	$19.99
00690901	Black Sabbath – Best of	$22.99
00691010	Black Sabbath – Heaven and Hell	$22.99
00690148	Black Sabbath – Master of Reality	$19.99
00690142	Black Sabbath – Paranoid	$17.99
00148544	Michael Bloomfield – Guitar Anthology	$24.99
00158600	Joe Bonamassa – Blues of Desperation	$24.99
00198117	Joe Bonamassa – Muddy Wolf at Red Rocks	$24.99
00283540	Joe Bonamassa – Redemption	$24.99
00358863	Joe Bonamassa – Royal Tea	$24.99
00690913	Boston	$19.99
00690491	David Bowie – Best of	$22.99
00286503	Big Bill Broonzy – Guitar Collection	$19.99
00690261	The Carter Family Collection	$19.99
00691079	Johnny Cash – Best of	$24.99
00690936	Eric Clapton – Complete Clapton	$34.99
00694869	Eric Clapton – Unplugged	$24.99
00124873	Eric Clapton – Unplugged (Deluxe)	$29.99
00138731	Eric Clapton & Friends – The Breeze	$24.99
00139967	Coheed & Cambria – In Keeping Secrets of Silent Earth: 3	$24.99
00141704	Jesse Cook – Works, Vol. 1	$19.99
00288787	Creed – Greatest Hits	$22.99
00690819	Creedence Clearwater Revival	$27.99
00690648	Jim Croce – Very Best of	$19.99
00690572	Steve Cropper – Soul Man	$22.99
00690613	Crosby, Stills & Nash – Best of	$29.99
00690784	Def Leppard – Best of	$24.99
00694831	Derek and the Dominos – Layla & Other Assorted Love Songs	$24.99
00291164	Dream Theater – Distance Over Time	$24.99
00278631	Eagles – Greatest Hits 1971-1975	$22.99
00278632	Eagles – Very Best of	$39.99
00690515	Extreme II – Pornograffiti	$24.99
00150257	John Fahey – Guitar Anthology	$24.99
00690664	Fleetwood Mac – Best of	$24.99
00691024	Foo Fighters – Greatest Hits	$24.99
00120220	Robben Ford – Guitar Anthology	$29.99
00295410	Rory Gallagher – Blues	$24.99
00139460	Grateful Dead – Guitar Anthology	$29.99
00691190	Peter Green – Best of	$24.99

00287517	Greta Van Fleet – Anthem of the Peaceful Army	$19.99
00287515	Greta Van Fleet – From the Fires	$19.99
00694798	George Harrison – Anthology	$24.99
00692930	Jimi Hendrix – Are You Experienced?	$29.99
00692931	Jimi Hendrix – Axis: Bold As Love	$24.99
00690304	Jimi Hendrix – Band of Gypsys	$24.99
00694944	Jimi Hendrix – Blues	$29.99
00692932	Jimi Hendrix – Electric Ladyland	$27.99
00660029	Buddy Holly – Best of	$24.99
00200446	Iron Maiden – Guitar Tab	$29.99
00694912	Eric Johnson – Ah Via Musicom	$24.99
00690271	Robert Johnson – Transcriptions	$27.99
00690427	Judas Priest – Best of	$24.99
00690492	B.B. King – Anthology	$29.99
00130447	B.B. King – Live at the Regal	$19.99
00690134	Freddie King – Collection	$22.99
00327968	Marcus King – El Dorado	$22.99
00690157	Kiss – Alive	$19.99
00690356	Kiss – Alive II	$24.99
00291163	Kiss – Very Best of	$24.99
00345767	Greg Koch – Best of	$29.99
00690377	Kris Kristofferson – Guitar Collection	$22.99
00690834	Lamb of God – Ashes of the Wake	$24.99
00690525	George Lynch – Best of	$29.99
00690955	Lynyrd Skynyrd – All-Time Greatest Hits	$24.99
00694954	Lynyrd Skynyrd – New Best of	$24.99
00690577	Yngwie Malmsteen – Anthology	$29.99
00694896	John Mayall with Eric Clapton – Blues Breakers	$19.99
00694952	Megadeth – Countdown to Extinction	$24.99
00276065	Megadeth – Greatest Hits: Back to the Start	$24.99
00694951	Megadeth – Rust in Peace	$27.99
00690011	Megadeth – Youthanasia	$24.99
00209876	Metallica – Hardwired to Self-Destruct	$24.99
00690646	Pat Metheny – One Quiet Night	$24.99
00102591	Wes Montgomery – Guitar Anthology	$27.99
00691092	Gary Moore – Best of	$27.99
00694802	Gary Moore – Still Got the Blues	$24.99
00355456	Alanis Morisette – Jagged Little Pill	$22.99
00690611	Nirvana	$24.99
00694913	Nirvana – In Utero	$22.99
00694883	Nirvana – Nevermind	$19.99
00690026	Nirvana – Unplugged in New York	$19.99
00265439	Nothing More – Tab Collection	$24.99
00243349	Opeth – Best of	$22.99
00690499	Tom Petty – Definitive Guitar Collection	$29.99
00121933	Pink Floyd – Acoustic Guitar Collection	$27.99
00690428	Pink Floyd – Dark Side of the Moon	$22.99
00244637	Pink Floyd – Guitar Anthology	$24.99
00239799	Pink Floyd – The Wall	$24.99
00690789	Poison – Best of	$22.99
00690925	Prince – Very Best of	$24.99
00690003	Queen – Classic Queen	$24.99
00694975	Queen – Greatest Hits	$25.99
00694910	Rage Against the Machine	$22.99
00119834	Rage Against the Machine – Guitar Anthology	$24.99
00690426	Ratt – Best of	$24.99
00690055	Red Hot Chili Peppers – Blood Sugar Sex Magik	$19.99

00690379	Red Hot Chili Peppers – Californication	$22.99
00690673	Red Hot Chili Peppers – Greatest Hits	$22.99
00690852	Red Hot Chili Peppers – Stadium Arcadium	$29.99
00690511	Django Reinhardt – Definitive Collection	$24.99
00690014	Rolling Stones – Exile on Main Street	$24.99
00690631	Rolling Stones – Guitar Anthology	$34.99
00323854	Rush – The Spirit of Radio: Greatest Hits, 1974-1987	$22.99
00173534	Santana – Guitar Anthology	$29.99
00276350	Joe Satriani – What Happens Next	$24.99
00690566	Scorpions – Best of	$24.99
00690604	Bob Seger – Guitar Collection	$24.99
00234543	Ed Sheeran – Divide*	$19.99
00691114	Slash – Guitar Anthology	$34.99
00690813	Slayer – Guitar Collection	$24.99
00690419	Slipknot	$19.99
00316982	Smashing Pumpkins – Greatest Hits	$22.99
00690912	Soundgarden – Guitar Anthology	$24.99
00120004	Steely Dan – Best of	$27.99
00322564	Stone Temple Pilots – Thank You	$22.99
00690520	Styx – Guitar Collection	$22.99
00120081	Sublime	$19.99
00690531	System of a Down – Toxicity	$19.99
00694824	James Taylor – Best of	$19.99
00694887	Thin Lizzy – Best of	$22.99
00253237	Trivium – Guitar Tab Anthology	$24.99
00690683	Robin Trower – Bridge of Sighs	$19.99
00156024	Steve Vai – Guitar Anthology	$34.99
00660137	Steve Vai – Passion & Warfare	$29.99
00295076	Van Halen – 30 Classics	$29.99
00690024	Stevie Ray Vaughan – Couldn't Stand the Weather	$19.99
00660058	Stevie Ray Vaughan – Lightnin' Blues 1983-1987	$29.99
00217455	Stevie Ray Vaughan – Plays Slow Blues	$24.99
00694835	Stevie Ray Vaughan – The Sky Is Crying	$24.99
00690015	Stevie Ray Vaughan – Texas Flood	$22.99
00694789	Muddy Waters – Deep Blues	$27.99
00152161	Doc Watson – Guitar Anthology	$24.99
00690071	Weezer (The Blue Album)	$22.99
00237811	White Stripes – Greatest Hits	$24.99
00117511	Whitesnake – Guitar Collection	$24.99
00122303	Yes – Guitar Collection	$24.99
00690443	Frank Zappa – Hot Rats	$22.99
00121684	ZZ Top – Early Classics	$27.99
00690589	ZZ Top – Guitar Anthology	$24.99

COMPLETE SERIES LIST ONLINE!

HAL•LEONARD®
www.halleonard.com

Prices and availability subject to change without notice.
*Tab transcriptions only.

0122
272